W9-BNB-693

CONCILIUM

Religion in the Seventies

CONCILIUM

New Series: Volume 10 Number 10: Moral Theology

SEXUALITY IN CONTEMPORARY CATHOLICISM

Edited by

Franz Böckle and Jacques-Marie Pohier

A CROSSROAD BOOK
The Seabury Press • New York

1976
The Seabury Press
815 Second Avenue
New York, N.Y. 10017

Library of Congress Catalog Card Number: 76-45528
ISBN: 0-8164-2097-1
Printed in the United States

CONTENTS

Editorial

SEX again! That will be the reaction of some readers who think that quite enough has been written and said on the subject. Others will be suprised that *Concilium* has waited ten years before dedicating an issue to it. Nevertheless, it is clearly a subject of considerable theoretical and practical importance in view of what is happening within the Catholic Church alone. The topic is in fact so vast and complex that we could only touch on one or two of its many aspects.

It proved impossible to undertake a serious study of all the problems of practical moral theology which are at present under discussion in matters of sex, even in the Catholic Church, whether at the instigation of believers who pose these problems out of faith, or as a result of debates and changes in laws and customs which occur outside but take effect within the Church.

It also proved impossible to present in any responsible way all the lessons and experiences of 20 centuries of Christianity: the inheritance of the Old and New Testaments, the Father of the Church, the great doctors of the Middle Ages, and all the centuries down to the present day. For that we would have needed an encyclopædia, all the more so because in these instances history and the final outcome should not be restricted to doctrine and theory, but should extend to social behavior and the everyday life of Christian men and women. All the violations of such conduct are far from well-known; they vary considerably, as far as one can tell, over the centuries, from place to place, from culture to culture, and from one social class to another.

It was also impossible to sum up all we have learned about sex in the last century or so. It is a commonplace to say that we have learnt more about sexuality in the last century than in all previous centuries, even if the theoretical and practical conclusions of that statement are rarely drawn. The extraordinary progress made in various branches of biology and in historical scholarship, the appearance and development of psychology and psychiatry, of sociology and ethnology, and so on, have offered findings which have hardly as yet begun (despite their radical importance and originality) to shape the general picture of sexuality.

Finally, it proved impossible to take into account in any truly representative sense a fact which is nevertheless borne witness to by all these disciplines: the meaning of sexuality and its ramifications and laws vary considerably from one society to another and from one age to another. Sex doesn't mean the same thing to the Bostonian upper middle-class that it means to a central African hunter, an Indonesian peasant, a Florentine aristocrat of the Quattrocento, or the Corinthians to whom St Paul was writing. Again, only an encyclopædia could satisfy the immense cultural variety of the topic.

In fact the present controversies on quite diverse subjects (contraception, abortion, divorce, pre-marital and extra-marital relations, priestly celibacy, 'eroticism', homosexuality, and so on) are so lively and so generalized that we tend to forget that a very short time ago almost all Catholics agreed among themselves and with the hierarchy on the general understanding of sex offered to them by Catholic teaching, and on almost all the moral, practical and legal consequences of that understanding. That agreement was so general that in many countries where Catholics were a minority, the most obvious sign of belonging to the Catholic community was to practise and acknowledge a view of sex in accordance with the demands of the Catholic Church.

In less than twenty years, however, the situation has changed completely. Catholics often disagree profoundly on most questions of sexual morality. Laymen and hierarchies are far from agreement, as was obvious in regard to *Humanae Vitae*. Priests are also divided. In the United States, for example, a large majority of priests consulted by their bishops in an extremely exacting inquiry came out against obligatory celibacy for priests, even though at the Roman Synod of 1971 all their bishops were in favour of retaining it. Sometimes the hierarchy itself was not unanimous. At the second Vatican Council the Holy See found the most prudent course was to withdraw from free discussion by the Fathers all those points of sexual morality which seemed controversial, and in Belgium recently one bishop refused to sign a letter on abortion signed and published by all other members of his episcopal conference.

What has happened? We can't wait the many years which historians require to explain such a phenomenon, because it is a question for us of living today and for tomorrow. Therefore we have to find what promotes a living faith and sexuality and what destroys them. That is the most urgent task.

However fast-moving and profound the crisis may be, there is no reason to despair. Christians pray, Christians love, Christians think. The Catholic community is not without problems but it is not without resources either. If we consider the matter without clarity, courage or faith, we are liable to see nothing but degradation and even tragedy. A healthy and holy emphasis will enable us to see things more positively. There are of course complex and decisive relations between sex and power (whether that power is economic, social, political, cultural or ecclesiastical), which require a political consideration of sexuality. But our too western, apolitical, and of course masculine and clerical approach is also characteristic of our church society and indeed of human society in general. We trust in the Spirit of God and ask him to remake the image of our Church, and of humankind as a whole.

FRANZ BÖCKLE
JACQUES-MARIE POHIER

Translated by John Maxwell

Peter Go

Sexuality in the Proclamation of Pius XII

MANY themes and topics associated with specific 'movements' within the Church have matured greatly since the time of Pius XII, and they found official confirmation in the pronouncements of Vatican II. That is the case with social issues, for example, and also with themes taken up by the liturgical movement, the ecumenical movement, and biblical studies. From the reign of Pius XII on, they have undergone steady elaboration and development. Such is not the case with the whole subject of sexuality. It was only after the time of Pius XII that it could be dealt with more openly and comprehensively, so that gradually certain features of the Church's basic position were subjected to re-examination and revision that went beyond a merely casuistic presentation of the traditional line of thought. But even here we note a certain restraint being imposed by Pope Paul VI.

The basic outlook and orientation of Pius XII came across pretty clearly in his own pronouncements. Insofar as that did not seem to suffice, he sought to get across his basic position by focusing on one main issue and hammering it home through the decisions of those organs of the curia that had competence in the matter. The issue in question was the end and purpose of marriage, which he saw as the supporting pillar of the whole doctrinal edifice concerned with this matter.[1] If we take a close look at the general atmosphere within the Church in his day, we can appreciate the range and import of this basic position insofar as contemporary Catholic sexual morality was concerned.

The other themes mentioned above had been under consideration for decades, thanks to the impetus given by special movements concerned with them. After the time of Pius XII, therefore, they reached a certain level of maturity and the ground had already been prepared for further exploration. That was not the case with the theme of sexuality. When it became a crucial issue after the time of Pius XII, the Church's position seemed not to have reached a satisfactory of level of development and maturity. For this reason the Church's pronouncements did not seem to be balanced and well-rounded. They repeatedly went back to the points laid down by Pius XII himself, which in turn represented a further development of his predecessor's teaching. Thus it does not seem to be an exaggeration to say that the pontificate of Pius XII represents a distinctive stage in the ongoing development of the Church's doctrine on sexuality.

During his almost twenty-year reign, which was marked by the upheavals of World War II and the postwar period, Pius XII repeatedly issued statements and pronouncements on marriage and sexuality. But it is worth noting that they seem to cluster around the early forties and fifties.[2] In this paper I shall try to present some of the most characteristic features of his pronouncements on sexuality. Firstly I shall present some elements of his basic underlying position concerning the norms governing sexuality. Then I shall consider his basic stance in evaluating the place of sexuality with the Christian dispensation, for that issue has receded into the background as specific questions about sexuality have become crucial ones in the present pastoral situation. Finally I shall try to sum up some features of Pius XII's distinctive outlook insofar as his pronouncements provide us with clues.

Taking an overall view, then, we can see that the first section moves on the plane of natural law for the most part while the second section is more concerned with specifically theological matters. It is taken for granted in church documents that marriage and sexuality are intrinsically ordered towards one another. This presupposition finds external expression in the fact that the two topics are frequently treated together in those documents. Since they cannot be isolated from one another, it is inevitable that we must consider documents which deal primarily with marriage or various forms of single life; for they often speak indirectly about sexuality as well. While marriage may stand in the foreground of attention in much of the treatment which follows, the reader should interpret my treatment insofar as it bears on the broader issue of sexuality.

One final observation is in order. I deliberately used the word 'proclamation' rather than 'teaching' in my title in order to bring out some of the flavor of the surrounding context. I have tried to help the reader to grasp something of the surrounding external atmosphere and the pastoral situation involved.[3]

I. CHARACTERISTIC FEATURES OF PIUS XII'S BASIC POSITION ON THE NORMS GOVERNING SEXUALITY

Three points will be considered in some detail under this heading: (1) the growing shift in stress from the earlier *bona* model to a *fines* model; (2) the canonical stamp of his first pronouncements which sought to spell out the ends of marriage; and (3) his view of the personal character of sexuality and its function of service.

Shift of emphasis from bona *to* fines

Ecclesial treatment of the complex issue of marriage has utilized two different models. Each model has certain inadequacies, so that the two have tended to complement one another. The *bona* model has concentrated on considering what 'goods' are served by marriage. The more recent *fines* model has concentrated on what 'ends' are served by marriage. These two models have been further complemented by a consideration of the essential features of marriage: oneness and indissolubility (see Code of Canon Law, canon 1013, n.2).

The *bona* model goes back to Augustine, and it originally provided an apology for sexual activity insofar as the basic evaluation of such activity was a negative one. Such activity was to be countenanced for the good of the offspring (*bonum prolis*), the good of the faith (*bonum fidei*— i.e., fidelity), and the good of the sacrament (*bonum sacramenti*— i.e., indissolubility). In the course of history the apologetic function eventually faded and the *bona* model was enriched with more solid and positive content. Such is the case especially in the encyclical *Casti connubii.*

The *fines* model deals with the ends of marriage: i.e., the procreation and upbringing of offspring (*procreatio atque educatio prolis*); mutual aid (*mutuum adiatorium*); and the healing of concupiscence (*remedium concupiscentiae*). On this see the Code of Canon Law, canon 1013, n.1, which will be cited as CIC hereafter.

Now the important point here is that these two models cannot be equated with each other. Materially speaking, they do not fully coincide. Moreover, two of the *bona* in the fist model (*bonum fidei* and *bonum sacramenti*) cannot be included under the 'ends' of marriage. And during the reign of Pius XII we note a marked shift in emphasis in church pronouncements, a shift which becomes all the more striking when we look at church pronouncements both before and after his reign. During his pontificate stress is placed more and more on the 'ends' of marriage. More and more it is the *fines* model that is used in treatments of marriage.

This striking shift often goes unnoticed because discussion of the ends of marriage is commonplace in our day. We do not realize how recent the use of the *fines* model is in pronouncements by the magisterium. But such use really does not go back further than the CIC (1917). Outside of the CIC one cannot find any important source that relies solidly on the *fines* model. A few sections in *Casti connubii* seem to move in that direction, but when we look at them closely we realize that they are conceived in accordance with the *bona* model. Much the same holds true for the CIC itself. When we look at the fonts cited by Gasparri in connection with canon 1013, n. 1, we find that they are heavily indebted to the *bona* model. Even after the time of Pius XII, the *bona* model seems to retain its hold. To cite but one example, Vatican II's declarations on marriage and sexuality evince great reluctance to use the *fines* model. Indeed we notice that the points brought to a fine edge by Pius XII in connection with that model are simply omitted.

The shift in emphasis from the *bona* model to the *fines* model takes place in the very first phase of Pius XII's pontificate. That phase coincides with the eruption of lively discussion and debate over the books published by H. Doms and B. Krempel. Indeed their publications can be regarded as the factor which triggered a response from the Church and led the magisterium to take a stand on the matter. Pronouncements on marriage and sexuality greatly increase in number and frequency, and they take a new direction. More and more they attempt to spell out the whole doctrine of the ends of marriage and its implicit content.

The canonical stamp of the first pronouncements on the ends of marriage

The proper hierarchy of marriage ends is treated expressly and in detail for the first time during the pontificate of Pius XII—both by himself and by by other official organs at his behest. This treatment stresses that the secondary ends of marriage are both dependent on, and subordinate to, the primary end of marriage. And it bears the strong imprint of canon law in its formulation.

The first important statement by Pius XII along these lines was his allocution to the Sacred Roman Rota on 3 October 1941. It was directly bound up with the canonical problem of physical impotence, which gave him an opportunity to spell out the proper hierarchy of marriage ends insofar as they were relevant in trying to determine the essential components of the act of procreation. Warning against one-sided emphases and stressing the need for proper balance, Pius XII spelled out some of the issues in greater detail but left it up to the Roman Rota to explore the underlying reasons and provide a complete elucidation of the matter.[4]

Before I go into the matter more deeply, I should like to sketch the main outlines of his basic position and its high points. A hierarchy of ends bespeaks dependence and some essential subordination. One may of course focus on the notion of dependence, as F. Hürth chooses to do; but even he is forced to admit that it is already implied in the notion of subordination.[5] This is also brought out in the commentary accompanying the decree of the Holy Office, which talks about various publications that maintain that the secondary ends of marriage are not subordinate to the primary end although they are dependent on the latter.[6] (Note the distinction set up between the two.)

Dependence implies a connection. In this case it is such that the dependent secondary end cannot exist without the primary end. Or, as Pius XII put it in one formulation, the secondary end cannot be separated or isolated from the primary end.[7]

But dependence can exist between two things on the same level and two things having the same value. The notion of subordination, then, goes further and implies that the secondary ends are meant to function in the service of the primary end. And here an important point is made about this subordination. The subordination in question is of an essential and metaphysical nature, so that the sexual act is endowed with the quality of inviolability. As F. Böckle puts it: "Thus the process of determining ends had now moved to a higher level, to a determination of the essential *metaphysical* character of the sexual act above and beyond any and all concrete physical possibilities. The Code of Canon Law (canon 1082, n. 2) defined the nature of the sexual act as one which in itself was suited to procreation (*actus per se aptus ad prolis generationem*). This meant nothing more and nothing less than that it could have a hand in procreation."[8] I shall come back to this point, but first I would like to pursue the line of thought contained in the Rota decision of 22 January 1944 and add a few observations of my own about the whole problem in question.

In trying to spell out the Church's teaching on the ends of marriage, the line of thought used bears the stamp of canon law and follows the *fines* model. This model now steps to center stage. When several *fines operis* are present, it is necessary to put them in order. One of these *fines* must be the specifying final cause which represents the primary aim or goal. The other ends are associated with, and contained in, the primary end so that the latter may be achieved more easily, certainly, and completely. In marriage this primary goal, which in and of itself specifies the nature of marriage ("*matrimonii naturam unice specificans*"), is the procreation and upbringing of offspring (nn. 10-11).

The decision then goes on to describe more exactly the proper relationship and ordering of marriage itself (nn. 12-13) and of the sexual act (nn. 14-16) to this primary end. Leaving aside the whole issue of the *opus naturae*, it describes the objective and natural ordering of marriage to the primary end in terms of what is necessary and sufficient by way of human action to effect the procreation and rearing of children in a way that is worthy of, and in line with, human nature. The underlying basis is the legal bond and commitment of the couple to perform acts which in themselves are suited to procreation.

This basic context is attributed to the act itself, so that the sexual or marital act is subordinated to the primary end of marriage. The Rota must have attached particular importance to this point because in one section (n. 16) it cites Pius XII as its chief witness; and it also alludes to the Rota decision of 25 April 1941, which dealt with the notion of an "*actus per se apti ad prolis generationem.*"

Here I should like to introduce some remarks on another issue: i.e., the whole problem of the relationship of canon law and moral theology to reality and of real life as the basis of their norms. As the reader will see, this will bring us back to the whole matter of an essential, metaphysical subordination of the secondary marriage ends to the primary end; and it will also bring us back to the "*actus per se apti ad prolis generationem.*"

Even in the early statements of Pius XII and the Rota alluded to above we note a curious thing. On the one hand they are very concerned to lay hold of reality as the solid bedrock of canonical norms. On the other hand this focus on reality takes a very pragmatic turn, so that it does not seem to be carried through in any consistent or thorough way.

A concern for concrete reality is evident in the many allusions to the natural and God-given order[9]; in the rejection of the assertion that different notions of the *potentia coeundi* are operative in biology, medicine, theology, and canon law and that the concept of canon law has nothing to do with natural law[10]; in the call for due consideration of medical opinions in cases concerned with the nullification of marriages[11]; and in the concern expressed in the line of argument that the 'effectibility' of the primary end be guaranteed.[12]

Yet this concern for reality is handled in a very pragmatic way. This shows up, for example, when canon law attempts to determine what conditions must be met if the marital right is to be translated into the performance of acts suited to procreation. The fact is that canon law is satisfied with very practical criteria in making this determination.[13] One cannot help but wonder if the concern for reality is a bit too abstract, half-hearted, and even one-sided when one reads the canonical discussion of the matter. For on the one hand it asserts that 'real semen' (*semen verum*) is required, but on the other hand it asserts that such matters as dead sperm, lifeless sperm, and insufficient sperm are irrelevant.[14]

No less instructive, it seems to me, is a statement in the Rota decision of 25 April 1941 to which explicit reference is made in the later decision of 22 January 1944 when it is talking about the whole matter of the relevance or irrelevance of reality. The concept of "*actus per se apti ad prolis generationem*" is not modified or cancelled out in any way by the findings of modern biology. Why? Because the various kinds of sperm discovered in the microscope are wholly alien to reality as that is defined and described by the sound common-sense judgment of mankind. The distinction between "*per se*" and "*per accidens*" must be based wholly on empirical observation when the Rota goes on to say that its definitions are concerned with what is present *per se*, not with what may be absent *per accidens*, and then spells out what "present *per se*" means by describing the *potentia coeundi* as it is generally understood by the sound and common-sense judgment of mankind.[15]

It need hardly be pointed out that this concept from canon law is understood in terms of natural law and is taken for granted in moral theology. J. Fuchs writes: "The *marriage law* of the Church speaks the same language. . . . It would be quite improper to regard the clearcut and straightforward marriage law of the Church as *nothing more* than a feasible ordering of the legal aspect. It would be improper not to view the term '*actus aptus ad generationem*' in its full and authentic sense, as it is regarded in moral theology. For in the whole question of sterility and impotence we are dealing with *natural law*, which must be taken up and integrated into marriage law."[16]

More than one theologican, however, has felt compelled to point out the problematic nature of this concept and explore it further.[17] Since a thorough exploration of the question would exceed the limits of this paper, I shall restrict myself to the following comments. Pius XII depicts the procreation process as a linked chain of causes ("*concatenazione delle cause*") with a clear-cut division of roles between nature and the human being. But he does not make it clear that the elements which are part and parcel of the *opus naturae*, and which are absolutely necessary *per se* rather than *per accidens* if procreation is to take place, are at man's disposal relatively infrequently. So while a distinction is made between the *opus naturae* and the *opus hominis* in the causal chain, they are equated for all practical purposes insofar as the *finis operis* is concerned. Though a distinction is introduced between *per se* and *per accidens*, it has nothing to do with real de facto procreation. The consideration of elements necessary for procreation focuses exclusively on one side of the equation, on the *opus hominis*, and disregards the required *opus naturae.*[18] That raises the question as to whether such a position, which suits the canonical frame of reference very well, is not to be traced back to a traditional biology and metaphysics of procreation in which the distinction between *per se* and *per accidens* is handled metaphysically.

In contrast to canon law, moral theology cannot rest content with determining the essential elements of the sex act by means of practical criteria. In fact it must operate very differently with the premises than does canon law. The perspective of canon law, conditioned by its basic concern to solve borderline cases, tends to convey the impression that it is inconsistent. To cite an example, I would point to the Rota decision of 22 January 1944. In one section (n. 21 ff.), it is talking about the relationship of a secondary end of marriage, mutual aid for the spouses, to the primary end of marriage. This secondary end and its corresponding right are grounded in the primary end and its corresponding right: "A natural consequence and complement flowing from this [primary] right is the [secondary] right to everything that is required if the right to bear and bring up a child is to be exercised in a way worthy of a human being. But it can only be exercised in this latter way if the right to mutual aid and support is joined to the basic primary right" (n. 22). However, after it has grounded this secondary end and right in the primary end and right, it goes on to draw a conclusion about what constitutes a valid marriage that rules out any practical implementation of the secondary right. "Since this subordinate right is not an essential, constitutive element of the primary right nor a necessary and indispensable precondition for it, a marriage can be entered legitimately on the basis of the primary right even if the secondary right is expressly excluded" (n. 24).[19]

The apparent lack of logical consistency should be clear enough. At one point the document stresses the necessity of the secondary end if the primary end is to be achieved in a decently human way. Yet later on, the latter feature is excluded from the essential nature of marriage. In moral theology, by contrast, the element of human dignity is put forward as a basic line of argument.

In this section I have sought to underline the strong stamp of canon law on the first ecclesial attempts to spell out the ends of marriage. It might be well to conclude with a quote from L.M. Weber: "This decree [on the ends of marriage] was wielded with a strict and heavy hand. Within the bounds of the Church it was stretched to cover any and every discipline that dealt with marriage. Even publications dealing with pastoral psychology were attacked if authors did not hold strictly to the formulation of the Code of

Canon Law, if they felt convinced they must offer a different view of marriage on the basis of their own particular discipline. Yet that certainly was not what the canonical experts had intended at all. At least that is not what one expert, Arthur Wynen, had had in mind when he rendered the famous Rota decision. In private conversations he expressed the view that it was completely unscientific to broaden the authority of canonical norms so that it also applied to other disciplines."[20]

The personal character of sexuality and its function of service

The long years of debate and discussion with his opponents had a positive impact on the development of Pius XII's own line of thought. His understanding of sexuality took on personalist overtones more and more as time went on. He kept filling out the material content of the secondary ends of marriage, opening up to the underlying desires of those with opposite views and trying to meet them half way. This line of development begins in 1941 with his warning against one-sidedness and his plea for balanced judgment.[21] It takes on more color with his stand against artificial insemination in 1949, in which he specifically alluded to the personal character of the marital act. And it was developed further in statements of his position that were made in 1951, 1953, and 1956.[22]

Let us take a look at the most important statement in this vein. It is his allocution to midwives in 1951, particularly the fourth section in which he talks about protecting the correct order of values and human dignity. Pius XII does not explicitly designate personal values— which would include marital love— as ends of marriage in the strict and technical sense. But for all practical purposes he does classify them as such insofar as he sees the proper hierarchical ordering of marriage ends jeopardized by the theses of his opponents. Their view, he feels, turns the hierarchy of values upside down. His use of the term 'values' (*valores*)[23] alongside the term 'ends' (*fines*) may also be regarded as an attempt at rapprochement. The use of the two terms together is very reminiscent of the two terms in the title of H. Doms' book, *Vom Sinn und Zweck der Ehe*.

In filling out the material content of the secondary ends of marriage, Pius XII also comes closer to the terminology and emphasis of his opponents insofar as he gives them a highly concrete and personalist cast. Here is a sample of this trend in the same document mentioned above: "It is not just the shared external act that has been placed in the service of posterity by the will of God and nature. It is also the whole range and richness of the human personality, of its intellectual and psychic reality, as that is intensified and deepened by marital love as such."[24]

This allusion to personality values represents a real advance in filling out the content of the secondary ends of marriage. It certainly is a great advance over what the Rota decision of 22 January 1944 had to say about *remedium concupiscentiae* and *mutuum adiutorium.* Particularly noteworthy is the fact that Pius XII ascribes these personality values to the marital act itself, so that his line of thought is strikingly close to that of H. Doms: "In and of its own nature the marital act is a personal activity, a cooperative and mutual action performed simultaneously by the spouses. Thanks to the nature of those involved and the distinctive quality of the act itself, it is an expression of mutual self-giving which, Scripture tells us, makes them 'two in one flesh'."[25]

So we see that Pius XII had some very positive things to say about the personal values embodied in sexuality. At the same time, however, they were left behind in the shadows when he argued his case for sexual ethics. In the latter context he gives very little attention to the place of personal values in the hierarchy of marriage ends— except when he uses them to argue against artificial insemination.

The priority of the primary end of marriage dominates Pius XII's line of argument. This becomes all the more apparent and striking when you compare his way of establishing norms for sexual ethics with the approach of numerous moral theologians. The latter use a line of argument which points to the expressive content of the marital act as a sign of unreserved, loving self-surrender in all its fullness.[26]

The dominant place of the primary end is also evident in his attitude towards natural methods of birth control. It is permissible to use such methods for the whole duration of one's marriage, he notes, but there must be serious reasons ("*seri motivi*") for this habitual use. They are not unobjectionable simply because they are natural, for there is a positive obligation to procreate bound up with the married state.[27]

In the light of this attitude, it seems to me that J. Ziegler goes overboard in his estimation of the radical shift implied in Pius XII's position. He suggests that for the first time the Church officially gave up its one-sided stress on procreation in discussing the ends of marriage; that Pius XII's position represents a 'Copernican revolution' in the Catholic teaching on marriage.[28] By the same token, I do not think we should underestimate the position worked out by Pius XII and regard it as little more than inconsistent.

Does Pius XII's position suggest not only a lack of balance but also a real lack of consistency and coherence? It is not easy to answer that question, particularly insofar as the linkup between the personal and the functional aspects of sexuality is concerned. We move into the area of linguistics and word usage when we attempt to find out if sexuality is accorded a playful aspect or a distinctive quality of its own in the teaching of Pius XII. The opinion of this author is that it would be almost unthinkable for Pius XII to dwell on the playful aspect of sexuality. Though he does recognize the personal values involved, the service function of sexuality dominates his thinking about it.

II. THE VALUE AND PLACE OF SEXUALITY WITHIN THE CHRISTIAN DISPENSATION

In statements whch are primarily concerned with justifying abstention from sexual activity for some ideal or indicated reason, we should naturally expect to find remarks that play down the value and importance of sexual activity. In such a context sexual activity will be 'relativized' and brought down a peg or two on the Christian scale of values. Consider the issues of virginity, celibacy, and Christian widowhood. Whatever their essential nature may be, and however much they may be accorded more positive value in the Christian scale of values, they all essentially involve a renunciation of sexual activity.

Here I am not concerned with those issues for their own sake. I bring them up because they have some correlation with sexuality. Discussions of such issues will entail some negative or positive evaluation of them vis-à-vis sexual activity, and so we can learn something about the speaker's understanding and appreciation of sexuality itself. But of course we must recognize that this is a more indirect approach, involving a certain amount of selectivity and potential one-sidedness.

The possibility of abstaining from sexual activity and the inculcation of this as an ideal already implies some hierarchical ranking of sexuality and marriage within the Christian dispensation. Specifically, it represents a playing down of their value and importance vis-à-vis sexual abstention. This finds clear expression in the fact that Pius XII placed marriage after virginity. As he himself acknowledges, he took advantage of every opportunity to reiterate and spell out the doctrine of Trent on this matter, and that doctrine stressed the superiority and priority of virginity and celibacy over marriage. Opposing currents of opinion eventually occasioned his encyclical entitled *Sacra Virginitas*.[29]

Now such a doctrine need not necessarily imply a devaluation of sexual activity and marriage. In and of itself it simply represents an attempt to put things in their proper place within an overall context or hierarchy. Pius XII himself, for example, complained that many people were deviating from the teaching of Trent and evaluating marriage so highly that their position came down to a denigration of virginity and ecclesiastical celibacy.[30] We might turn his objection around, however, and suggest that his exaltation of virginity (in his encyclical and elsewhere) came down to a denigration of marriage and sexual activity.

In any case we cannot decide the matter on a priori grounds. So let us take a closer look at what Pius XII had to say.

Sexuality vis-à-vis virginity and celibacy

In his encyclical on virginity Pius XII offers a variety of overlapping reasons for the priority of virginity. But he himself stresses one particular reason: "Virginity is preferable to marriage then, as We have said, above all else because it has a higher aim—that is to say, it is a very efficacious means for devoting oneself wholly to the service of God, while the heart of married persons will remain more or less 'divided'."[31] This passage reveals the general structure of his argument. Marriage in general is played down or 'relativized'. This in turn leads to a playing down of all its specific aspects and features in and through the same line of argument, which focuses on *the relative worth of the aims or goals involved.* This 'duality' pervades his whole treatment of the issues in this encyclical.

To begin with, the sexual instinct is played down and made subordinate to the instinct for self-preservation. Pius XII rejects the notion that the sexual instinct is the most important and powerful one in man, and the attendant conclusion that man cannot restrain it for a whole lifetime without danger to his vital nervous system and the harmonious development of his personality. In so doing, Pius XII appeals expressly to the teaching of Thomas Aquinas regarding the proper order of natural instincts and inclinations. Even on the basic natural level shared by other animals and human beings, the instinct for self-preservation comes first. Moreover, the function of the rational faculty, which is the distinguishing mark of human nature, is to regulate those fundamental instincts and thereby ennoble them.[32] However much one may agree with the notion that man's natural instincts must be properly ordered, the repeated reference to 'ennobling' in the encyclical does suggest a conception of sexuality that is not too positive.

At this point the possibility of the human subject controlling the sexual instinct is in turn relativized and played down because Pius XII introduces a theological note which suggests that man cannot handle the objective activity too well. Because of original sin, man may all too easily go overboard.[33] The higher aim is lost from view: "Nevertheless, it must be equally admitted that as a consequence of the fall of Adam the lower faculties of human nature are no longer obedient to right reason, and may involve man in dishonorable actions. As the Angelic Doctor has it, the use of marriage 'keeps the soul from full abandon to the service of God'."[34] If we go to the trouble of looking up the passage of Aquinas (Summa Th., II-II, q. 186, a.4), we find that he offers two reasons why the marriage act hinders wholehearted service to God. One reason goes back to Aristotle and Augustine—particularly the latter, whose teaching on marriage was closely bound up with the doctrine of original sin. It stresses the vehement nature of sexual pleasure itself. The second reason stresses the obligations of family life as alluded to by St. Paul (1 Cor. 7:32).

Pius XII does point out that Christ's grace has been given to us so that we may gain control over our corporeal faculties and passions, so that we may keep our bodies in subjection and live by the spirit. His reference to Paul's epistles (Gal. 5:25; 1 Cor. 9:29) is curious, however, because he takes Paul's contrast between the flesh and the spirit and restricts it to the sexual domain! We do find an appraisal of man's sexual activity here that is not altogether negative: "The virtue of chastity does not mean that we are insensible to the urge of concupiscence, but that we subordinate it to reason and the law of grace, by striving wholeheartedly after what is noblest in human and Christian life."[35]

A serious playing down of sexuality occurs when he talks about the role of marriage and sexual activity in personality growth and development. Here virginity is held up as the ideal. It is virginity that enables the soul to reign fully over the body and live a spiritual life in complete peace and freedom. Hence it is virginity which offers the greatest promise of personality fulfillment and perfect growth.[36]

A rather remarkable attitude towards sexual activity is revealed when Pius XII comes to talk about the reasons justifying celibacy. Sacred ministers do not renounce marriage solely because of their apostolic ministry but also because of their service at the altar. But note the line of reasoning he gives: "For if even the priests of the Old Testament had to abstain from the use of marriage during the period of their service in the Temple, for fear of being declared impure by the Law just as other men, is it not much more fitting that the ministers of Jesus Christ, who offer every day the Eucharistic Sacrifice, possess perfect chastity?"[37] In alluding to the priests of the Old Testament, a whole series of texts are cited for support: Lev. 15:16-17; 22:4; 1 Sam. 21:5-7; see Siric. Papa, Ep. ad Himer. 7; P.L., LVI, 558-559. Not only does the reasoning behind the Old Testament prohibition go unchallenged, it is applied a fortiori to the situation of priests in the Roman Catholic Church. Yet if we take the trouble to look at the sources cited, we find that a whole series of varied sexual and purely physiological processes are involved, and they range from the spilling of semen to skin diseases.

Sexuality vis-à-vis Christian widowhood

In vain does one look for a positive statement about entering a second marriage. The most one can find is a grudging refusal to pass judgment on someone who remarries after the death of a spouse. Yet even those statements are usually ancillary to some main statement which expresses a deep and abiding preference for Christian widowhood.[38]

This preference for Christian widowhood carries all before it. In talking about other issues such as the ends of marriage or divorce,[39] for example, Pius XII will often stress the importance of the parents' role in the upbringing of children. Yet when he comes to discuss widowhood and possible remarriage, the importance of this educational role does not enter the picture at all.

What about the 'incomplete' family, then? What about the family that now lacks a father, for example? Pius XII resolves the problem by saying that the widowed mother should now take on the father role as well, rather than providing her children with a new father through remarriage. She is to provide her children with a male image as well, and with a virile upbringing: "The widow will undoubtedly consecrate herself to her duty as educator with all the delicacy and tactfulness of a mother, but will remain united in spirit to her husband, who will suggest to her in God the attitudes she must take, and will give her authority and discernment."[40]

According to Pius XII, Christian widowhood means fidelity to the male partner beyond the grave. Death can strengthen and perfect the bonds of human and supernatural love between them. Hence death becomes a process of purification through which the spouses are released from their bodily attachments, their traces of egotism, and their physical weaknesses. The dead spouse invites the partner left on earth to enter a more pure and spiritual state of mind: "Since one of the spouses has consummated his sacrifice, should not the other be willing to detach herself more from the world, and to renounce the intense but fleeting joys of sensible and carnal affection which bound the husband to the home and monopolized her heart and energies? By accepting the cross of separation, and by renouncing the presence of her dear one, another presence is gained which is more intimate, more profound, and stronger. It is a purifying presence also."

The theological basis of this line of thought is the sacrament of marriage insofar as it symbolizes the love relationship between Christ and his Church. That sacrament transfigures husband and wife so that he becomes similar to Christ and she to the Church redeemed by his sacrifice. Widowhood thus becomes "the natural outcome of this mutual consecration... awaiting the final fulfillment" after death. That is the greatness of widowhood "when it is lived as a prolongation of the graces of matrimony and as a preparation for their flowering in the light of God." The ideal, clearly enough, is a totally spiritualized marriage.[41]

III. CLUES TO PIUS XII'S OUTLOOK

In this very brief section I simply want to provide readers with some possible clues to Pius XII's overall outlook on sexuality. Without attempting to draw any definitive conclusions, I would say that the following observations deserve some consideration:

1. When we read the statements and publications of Pius XII, we can hardly avoid the impression that he attached great significance to sexual questions. Quantitatively, he devotes a large number of documents to sexual matters. Qualitatively, he explores issues in detail and often formulates a definitive position of his own.
2. When he begins to talk about ethical or moral lapses, or to warn people against them in his discurses, he will frequently cite the whole area of sexual behavior as an example of what he means.[42]
3. He reacted strongly and vehemently against the whole movement of sexual enlightenment in all its forms.[43]
4. His rigorous severity in this area may be explained by the fact that he linked sexuality up with the whole matter of salvation.[44]
5. His solemn stress and reiterated emphasis on the full application of the commandment of purity, "in all its gravity and seriousness," to the adolescent years still raises doubts as to whether he had given sufficient consideration to the findings of developmental psychology concerning adolescent sexuality.[45]
6. His linking of the quest for autonomy in sexual behavior with egotism and hedonism may stem from a justifiable concern for human beings or a mistrust and lack of confidence in them.[46]
7. In talking about sexual matters and sexual terms, he has a tendency to shift from Latin to French in the midst of one and the same talk. This hardly seems necessary to today's reader.[47]

Taken by themselves, these points may not seem to hold much weight. But when we put them all together, they do suggest an attitude towards sexuality which is worthy of note.

Translated by John J. Drury

Notes

1. This rather extensive note attempts to point up the role of Pius XII by presenting a brief chronology of the interplay between him and certain curial organs. Their pronouncements embody the process of action and reaction in the Church's evolving stance.

In the late thirties and early forties, debates over the books published by Doms and Krempel prompted the magisterium to take a stand on the issues raised:

— On 3 October 1941, Pius XII asked the Roman Rota to make a thorough study of certain questions dealing with marriage. See A.A.S., 1941, 33:412-426; on the ends of marriage see page 423.
— On 22 January 1944, the Rota presented its response to Pius XII's earlier request. See A.A.S., 1944, 36:184-193 in particular.
— On 10 March 1944, Pius XII apparently clarified his own stand. For some inexplicable reason this document cannot be found, though he himself alludes to it in his allocution of 29 October 1951 (see A.A.S., 1951, 43:849). Or else it is in fact identical with the decree of the Holy office dated 1 April 1944, as F. Hürth thinks (see *De re matrimoniali. Texta et documenta* 30 [Rome 1955], p. 120). Telling against any formal identity of the two is the fact that a few lines later Pius XII expressly alludes to the decree of the Holy Office. Thus footnote 20 in the 1951 text (A.A.S., 43:849) does not apply to his own clarification of 10 March 1944.
— On 20 March 1944, Pius XII approves the decree of the Holy Office on the ends of marriage that was issued on March 1 of that year (see A.A.S., 1944, 36:103).

In the early fifties statements were issued concerning the *amplexus reservatus* that was being discussed in France. The Lutheran bishops of Sweden also issued an epistle on sexual questions:

— On 29 October 1951, Pius XII delivers his address to midwives. See A.A.S., 1951, 43:835-854.
— Previously, on 18 September 1951, he had delivered an address to French fathers of families. See A.A.S., 1951, 43:730.
— On 30 June 1952, the Holy Office issues a warning against the use of the *amplexus reservatus* at the express request of Pius XII. See A.A.S., 1952, 44:546.

2. See note 1.

3. This is done in the introductory section, in the concluding summary, and *passim* throughout the article.

4. See A.A.S., 1941, 33:421-426, especially pages 423-424. Actually all that Pius XII explicitly asked the Rota to do in this instance was to carefully examine the conditions permitting the dissolution of a valid marriage. Noting the way he had spoken about the ends of marriage, however, the Rota took this as a request to explore that topic more deeply. On the occasion of a specific canonical case, therefore, it spelled out the hierarchy of marriage ends. This decision *coram Wynen* of 22 January 1944 implies a further exploration and study of the declaration which Pius XII made to the Rota on 3 October 1941. See A.A.S., 1944, 36:184, 187.

Statements and decisions of the Rota are introduced in this paper because Pius XII himself acknowledged their weight and importance. He noted that the decisions of that judicial body were greatly respected by moralists and jurists. For that reason the Rota had a serious obligation to uphold and interpret the legal norms in accordance with the mind of the Pope, because it performed its function as an organ of the Holy See under his control. This was particularly true in marriage cases. See A.A.S., 1941, 33:427.

5. See the additional comments on the decree *de finibus matrimonii* which are attributed to F. Hürth, in *Per. de re mor. can. lit.*, 1944, 33:220.

6. A.A.S., 1944, 36:103.

7. *Ibid.*, 1941, 33:423.

8. Afterword in Franz Böckle and Carl Holenstein (editors), *Die Enzyklika in der Diskussion. Eine orientierende Dokumentation zu 'Humanae vitae'* (Zurich-Einsiedeln-Cologne, 1968), p. 202.

9. These references are scattered throughout his talks and writings, and they are quite typical of his thinking. Pius XII repeatedly points out that God has arranged everything wisely for man's benefit and welfare. Hence man should respect the order established in nature. Only in that way can he ensure his own welfare and act in a morally upright way. In short, there is a correspondence between *bonum morale* on the one hand and *bonum physicum* on the other.

10. A.A.S., 1953, 45:677.

11. *Ibid.*, pp. 675-676.

12. See the Rota decision of 22 January 1944, nn. 10-11; A.A.S., 1944, 36:185.

13. A.A.S., 1953, 45:677.

14. Rota decision of 22 January 1944, n. 16; A.A.S., 1944, 36:187; see also A.A.S., 1953, 45:677.

15. Rota decision of 25 April 1941: "His suppositis apparet, quomodo 'actus per se apti ad prolis generationem', de quibus in can. 1081, n. 2, intelligi et describi debeant. Videlicet illi actus sunt *per se* apti ad prolis generationem, qui ponuntur a viro, testiculis (vel saltem uno testiculo) et canalibus perviis praedito, atque habili ad erectionem membri, ad penetrationem vaginae et ad effusionem seminis in vagina, licet *per accidens* semen careat elemento praecipuo id est nemaspermatibus: definitiones namque fiunt secundum ea quae *per se adsunt*, neglectis iis quae *per accidens deficiunt*" (*S.R. Decisiones seu sententiae*, 1941, 33:292-293).

16. J. Fuchs, "Biologie und Ehemoral," in *Greg.*, 1962, 43:240.

17. See H. Doms, *Gatteneinheit and Nachkommenschaft* (Mainz, 1965); and the summary overview by F. Böckle in the volume which he edited, *Das Naturrecht im Disput* (Düsseldorf, 1966), pp. 136-137.

18. A.A.S., 1951, 43:835 ff.

19. A.A.S., 1944, 36:188-189.

20. L.M. Weber, "Zur Interpretation kirchlicher Dokumente über den finis matrimonii," in *Theol. d. Geg.*, 1965, 8:147.

21. A.A.S., 1941, 33:423.

22. A.A.S., 1951, 43:848 ff; *Ibid.*, 1953, 45:677; *Ibid.*, 1956, 48:469-470.

23. A.A.S., 1951, 43:848 ff.

24. A.A.S., 1951, 43:849-850. When I talk about a rapprochement in emphasis between Pius XII and other writers, I am talking about such statements as these made by him: "If this relative valuation simply means that more stress should be placed on the personality of the spouses than on the personality of the child, then we might let the matter rest there, strictly speaking" (A.A.S., 1951, 43:848).

25. A.A.S., 1951, 43:850.

26. See the report of F. Böckle on the birth-control debate with the Church in *Concilium* 1, 1965 (Eng. trans., Paulist Press). Also see A. Valsecchi, *Regolazione delle nascite. Un decennio di riflessione teologiche* (3rd edition, Brescia, 1968).

27. A.A.S., 1951, 43:844-845.

28. J. Ziegler, "Menschliche Geschlechtlichkeit zwischen Emanzipation und Integration," in *Theol. u. Glaube*, 1974, 64:196.

29. A.A.S., 1954, 46:174. From 1954 on, English translations of all important papal documents can be found in *The Pope Speaks Magazine*, cited as TPS hereafter; in this case see TPS, 1954, 1:101-123.

30. *Ibid.*, 46:163.

31. *Ibid.*, pp. 170; TPS, 1:108.

32. *Ibid.*, pp. 174-175; TPS, 1:111.

33. *Ibid.*, p. 175.

34. *Ibid.*, p. 169; TPS, 1:107.

35. *Ibid.*, p. 175; TPS, 1:111.

36. *Ibid.*, pp. 175-176.

37. *Ibid.*, pp. 169-170; TPS, 1:108.

38. A.A.S., 1957, 49:900.

39. To give one example here, the upbringing of children as a primary end of marriage is often adduced in questions of sexual ethics as an argument against extramarital sex (see A.A.S., 1956, 48:471-473). The same basic argument that children need their parents is also used as an argument against divorce (see *Discorsi e radiomessaggi*, IV, 56). But if those factors are really so important, then they also speak in favor of a second marriage.

40. A.A.S., 1957, 49:903; TPS, 4:291. The full text is in TPS, 4:287-292.

41. *Ibid.*

42. A.A.S., 1950, 42:784-792.

43. A.A.S., 1951, 43:732-734; also A.A.S., 1950, 42:788-789.

44. A.A.S., 1950, 42:789-790.

45. A.A.S., 1952, 44:275-276.

46. A.A.S., 1951, 43:852-853.

47. A.A.S., 1956, 48:471-473.

Pierre de Locht

Conjugal Spirituality Between 1930 and 1960

IN this volume devoted to sexuality, the editors chose to characterize the period between 1930 and 1960 by focussing on 'conjugal spirituality'. It was a judicious choice for the period extending roughly from the date of *Casti connubii* (31 December 1930) to the years immediately prior to the opening of Vatican II. For it was precisely in terms of conjugal spirituality that Catholic circles lived the reality of their sexual lives during that period.

I. BRIEF CHRONOLOGICAL OVERVIEW

The thirties

I myself am not a firsthand witness to developments which took place between 1930 and 1940. But when I did begin to become increasingly involved in the family apostolate immediately after World War II, many echoes and vestiges of that earlier period remained. They indicated that the first stirrings of a new awareness about marriage had already begun to circulate through certain circles; and though these circles were still relatively limited in numbers, they were quite active and committed.

It was during the thirties that there arose the first stirrings of family action concerned with educating people in family life and reclaiming for the family its proper place and role. In France the Association du mariage chrétien was founded under the strong and forceful personality of Canon Viollet. It was also the period of the first books on conjugal spirituality by Père Carré and A. Christian,[1] which stressed the grandeur of marriage as a sacrament and the sacred companionship involved. And the first family-circle groups (*groupes de foyers*) also appeared.

This renewal took place chiefly under the impetus of Catholic Action. Many Catholics had discovered a militant and committed form of Catholicism when they had joined various youth movements such as the Y.C.W. Now, as adults, they wanted to continue living this ideal of an activist faith and holiness within the context of their married lives.

It is important to note that this burning desire to live a fully Christian life in the state of marriage came from the laity themselves, and that it arose out of renewed attention to the human reality of their day-to-day lives. Women as well as men dedicated themselves to this movement, operating on a level of equality as they had done in the youth organizations of their earlier school years. In the latter organizations women had not taken part primarily as future wives and mothers but as equally dedicated partners in community life and its responsibilities. The renewed interest in marriage and marital life arose out of this context, and the latter gave it certain distinctive features and characteristics. One cannot overlook these facts if one wishes to truly grasp the dynamism and exigencies of the renewal.

From this period date the first explicit challenges to the hierarchy regarding the ends of marriage. Paying closer attention to the reality of their daily lives, couples began to question the hierarchical view which gave complete priority to procreation, to the begetting and rearing of children. In their personal lives many spouses were already harmonizing and balancing the various finalities of marriage in a way which was at variance with the persistent teaching of the Church. Who would not be disturbed by the sight of a young man and woman getting married in order to have children, and not first and foremost because they loved each other and wanted to live their lives together! This gap between real-life experience and the official teaching of the Church was bridged more or less successfully, and often quite harmoniously, in the concrete life of the married couple. But it was difficult, if not downright impossible, to raise questions on the level of basic principles at this point in time—though that is precisely what H. Doms attempted to do in his work on the meaning and purpose of marriage.[2]

On more than one level the papal encyclical *Casti connubii* had been a positive stimulus. Reread some twenty or more years later, it might well seem to be heavily marked by the context of its own time,[3] but the early pioneers in the family movement saw it as something which rehabilitated human love, and Pius XI did indeed highlight the nobility and sanctity of that love when lived in the sacrament of the New Law known as Christian Matrimony.

The war years

World War II brought an abrupt halt to many external activities and initiatives. For many it was a time of inner exploration and renewal, a time for reflection on the essentials insofar as they related to personal and group life. A new stage was being prepared that would be marked by an intense desire to live and act and exist in a fuller and more authentic way.

The prolonged absence of large numbers of men and husbands permitted many women to give a fuller measure of their talent and energy to the tasks at hand. They shouldered important responsibilities in both the family and the social sector, and they acquired greater autonomy. In that epoch of widespread insecurity the family came to seem more precious than ever. But a whole new outlook regarding the proper division of tasks and interpersonal relationships was taking shape.

During this same period countless men experienced separation, danger, a gap in their emotional and sexual lives, and the loss of a stable, heartwarming milieu. They yearned to recover or create such a milieu for themselves. On a somewhat reworked foundation they would try to establish a locale for intimacy, dialogue, self-fulfillment, and responsible living of a truly human cast.

The postwar era

From 1945 on we find a rapid growth in family-circle groups and other initiatives of the same kind. They helped to bring out clearly the fact that the married couple is the crucial nucleus of family life, and that the unity and value of the home is conditioned and sustained primarily by the depth and intensity of the conjugal bond.

This new awareness was quite a novel one in human history. Up to that point social and even economic reasons had played a preponderant role in the stability of a family. But more and more people began to sense that only the quality and depth of the love shared by the spouses could guarantee a marriage and weld a family together. In many instances the welfare of the children was no longer enough to justify the continuation of a home life in which there was no real understanding between the couple. Many came to the conclusion that separation would be better for the children also, that it would be preferable to a facade of conjugal unity. This conclusion became more and more widespread. *We find a new emphasis on the married couple, their mutual self-fulfillment, and their conjugal spirituality.*

Growth and self-fulfillment. In the official doctrine of the Church at least, mutual growth and self-fulfillment had been considered a secondary item up to that time.[4] Indeed it was even considered to be somewhat tainted with egotism by comparison with the primary purpose of marriage: i.e., the unselfish procreation and rearing of children. Now the mutual growth and self-fulfillment of the couple became a priority issue.

This change in outlook was not due to any significant disregard for the role and the values of marriage. Married couples simply came to see that their love was the primary thing; that it was their love for each other that had created their marriage; and that their fecundity made sense only insofar as it was the joint realization and embodiment of mutual self-giving. Many came to see that procreation summoned them to fashion a marital community between themselves, to help each other as spouses, and to nurture each other's growth and personal self-fulfillment. Thus it was the mutual growth and fulfillment of the spouses that served as the foundation for marriage and the family. The spouses had to grow and develop as man and woman, and it was the deepening bond of love between them that would endow their conjugal community with indissolubility and creativity.

In this context their sexual relationship took on new importance. Many came to see it as a specific and distinctive locus of conjugal dialogue. Bodily union and harmony became an essential condition underlying the life and stability of the married couple. There was now to be a guest for complete sexual equality in their bodily dialogue since the female has the same sort of desires, the same right to show initiative and be active, and the same right to obtain physical fulfillment.

During this period, which was highlighted by the appearance of the Kinsey Report, we find people justifying physical pleasure and gratification as a real positive value in marital life, not just as something to which the couple has a right. There were the books written by Paul Chanson, for example. While they aroused much opposition, they certainly did help people to take due cognizance of the body and its possibilities for fulfillment. Apart from his discussion of the *amplexus reservatus*, the restrained approach to orgasm derived from oriental practice, Chanson was primarily concerned with a truly incarnate emphasis on marital life. He stressed the necessity of making their bodily union more human; the obligation of the husband to take greater pains to ensure sexual fulfillment for his spouse; the importance of striving for a bodily union that would truly 'monogamize' their love; and the importance of developing temperance and moderation in the actual exercise of sexual intercourse rather than simply through abstinence. Those were some of the values which Paul Chanson stressed with vigor and lyricism in his conferences with married couples and in his writings. It was an apostolate designed to foster the humanization of conjugal life.

Chanson's crusade provoked loud and stormy protest and debate. That would lead to astonishment and outright scandal when certain theologians, Père Feret in particular, offered theological support for his position. In his postscript to one of Chanson's books,[5] Feret would say that "in the concrete, there is not and cannot be any opposition or dissimilarity between the conjugal love of spouses and their charity-based love" (p. 135). Furthermore it is "their community of life, not any of its elements considered in isolation, that has as its primary aim the procreation and rearing of children" (p. 140). Rejecting a fatalistic view of the sexual instinct, to which only sexual abstinence would offer a satisfactory response, the married couple must learn how to develop temperance; but one is quite wrong if one equates temperance with continence. When one abstains from sexual intercourse, "the lower drives persist in a state of anarchic effervescence." Temperance, by contrast, does not disregard or neglect the rich resources of the senses and sense life, which are precious "even for the most spiritual of loves"; but it does render them "fully and amicably submissive to the spirit" (p. 146). Over against a pessimistic view of sexuality, this new point of view stressed the legitimate joy of loving with one's whole body and being.

Leaving aside the matter of the *amplexus reservatus* and its possible value for cementing the bodily union of the couple, we can say that it was the rehabilitation of physical union that assumed importance in the eyes of many people. Sexuality, then, was not simply an uncontrollable force whose vehemence could only be channelled into a groove or framework that made it legitimate; it was a precious component of the couple's communal life. While it would take much effort, they were to integrate it harmoniously into their joint effort and make the joy of loving a part of their life and existence.

It has never been made quite clear whether the warnings and subsequent crackdowns of the Holy Office[6] were directed specifically against the notion of the *amplexus reservatus* alone or against a broader line of thought. But it seems much more probable that they were directed against the new viewpoints concerning the role of sexuality in the life of the couple and the proper hierarchy of ends. The theses of Paul Chanson, and the supporting statements of more than one well known theologian,[7] certainly did provoke lively opposition among Christians and overly facile partisanship on occasion. But most of all Chanson helped to arouse a new awareness of the sexual dimension and its rightful place in the Christian ideal of marriage.

This rather detailed consideration of Paul Chanson and his work is not meant to suggest that he was an isolated figure making his own distinctive but lonely contribution. The fact is that in the late forties and early fifties we find a broad current of thought moving in the same direction.[8]

Conjugal spirituality. This new cognizance of the positive value of the body and sexuality could not have come about and won acceptance except for the fact that it appeared within a context which exalted conjugal spirituality and sought to shore up the institutional framework in which people were living their sexual lives. The link between spirituality on the one hand and sexual fulfillment on the other took on great importance during this period. It enabled many husbands and wives to take the risk of accepting and welcoming bodily love-making. For now they could find a place for that in an overall context which reinforced their oneness as a couple and nurtured their concern for sanctification through prayer and the apostolate. It is no accident that major family-life movements appeared on the scene at this point and grew impressively. For these movements helped spouses to discern and elaborate a lofty spirituality centered around their love and practiced within their highly incarnate state of life.

The stress was on spirituality in the Equipes Notre-Dame. Action was more central in the Christian Family Movement. The close tieup with day-to-day concerns was more characteristic of the Feuilles Familiales (Belgium) and the publications of the Association du mariage chrétien (France). But in all of them we find the same basic concern of people to harmonize the various and different components of the human reality that dominates their own lives; and in their view it was Christian marriage which would provide them with the best framework for doing just that and thereby achieving fulfillment. Indeed some people involved with these movements would go so far as to look for some ideal of total fusion in marriage, feeling that the individual personalities of the husband and the wife were fused into a new entity: the conjugal couple.

II. MAJOR CONCERNS OF MARRIED COUPLES

As the focus shifted to the couple in this period and as a new concern for conjugal spirituality developed, certain major concerns came to be voiced by family movements and the couples themselves. We can group them into certain basic categories.

Need for marital dialogue

How were husband and wife to truly encounter each other despite their differences—or even with the help of those differences? In some sectors or environments emphasis would be placed on fighting "the silence that murders love." From that stemmed the idea of the Equipes Notre-Dame to inculcate the obligation of sitting down and talking. Though some felt that their systematization of this approach was too artificial, it certainly did help many couples to learn how to talk to each other. In talking to another person we gain a greater awareness of ourselves, learn to hear and accept the other person as he or she is, and discover his or her most personal aspirations even though they may have been unknown to the speaker.

This approach, however, is probably more typical and necessary for a particular social category. While some spouses might benefit from being forced to sit down and talk to each other, couples in other circumstances would be more likely to deepen their communication by carrying out certain activities together. But all couples soon discover that shared responsibilities, even such fundamental ones as the procreation and rearing of children, do not automatically produce or guarantee their unity as a couple.

More and more it came to seem that sexual intercourse was truly the privileged locale for conjugal encounter and interpersonal dialogue. But obviously the language of sex had its own difficulties and inhibitions. The couple would have to learn this language slowly and patiently. Above and beyond merely superficial satisfaction, the quality of their sexual encounter and union would reveal the reality of their whole conjugal life.

Marital sexuality and procreation

Once married people came to experience sexual intercourse as a positive value enhancing their communion and fidelity, they and eventually moral theology would inevitably have to ask what was the proper balance between the various ends of marriage. Abstention from physical pleasure and gratification might readily have seemed commendable to an earlier day, but one could not so easily justify the renunciation of something which has great value in cementing the unity and cohesion of the married couple.

This somewhat novel perception of sexual intercourse as a marital language all its own went hand in hand with a rapid change in the birth rate and the size of families, and the two were not unconnected. In the space of a few short years after World War II, family size dropped sharply. Where once families of eight, ten, or even fourteen children were not rare, we now find families averaging three, four, or five children.

As yet there was no thought of calling into question the view that procreation constituted the primary purpose of marriage—at least on the level of theory and church principles. But it now seemed most important that the goals of marital communion and mutual self-fulfillment not be subordinated or sacrificed to procreation.

It is impossible to close one's eyes to the serious tension felt by many young couples as they seek to set up a balanced home life. They want to safeguard the fervor and equilibrium of their love and, at the same time, they want to produce a family that fits in with their own capacities and the needs of the children they will have. Food, housing, financial resources, psychological capacity, and educational capabilities must be taken into due consideration.

During this period countless discussions, investigations, and publications would be devoted to the problems of birth control,[9] even while the priority of the primary goal of marriage would stay firmly entrenched at the center of the Church's official teaching. In this atmosphere many would come to regard Pius XII's address to Italian midwives in October 1951[10] as a major turning point. While firmly recalling the traditional hierarchy of marriage ends and clearly reaffirming that the integrity of the conjugal act must be respected absolutely, he alluded to circumstances which might validly dispense one from the duty of procreation. To be sure, one was only permitted to take advantage of infertile periods. But at that point his affirmation of a legitimate form of birth control was of greater import than the restrictions surrounding it.

The search for a concrete solution would move towards center stage. Some, such as Henry Dumery for example, would point out that any and every method or technique is a two-edged weapon. "It can be used for good or ill. Only conscience, which gives rise to it, can pass judgment on it; it must never be dissociated from conscious awareness."[11]

Anxious to remain faithful to the teaching of the Church, however, many couples were led to center their concern for morally upright behavior on the choice of method more than on the broad and basic orientation of their love. The means became *ends in themselves*, with a moral value of their own, rather than remaining means to ends *which would confer a moral character on them.*

A specifically marital spirituality

A new and revitalized theology of the sacraments in general produced a new and revitalized theology of the sacrament of marriage. In the latter many Christian spouses now found the tieup between prayer and concrete life, between the profane world and the supernatural order, between their own love and the divine love revealed to us.

Much stress was now placed on the fact that the married spouses were the ministers of the marriage sacrament and remained so throughout their married lives. Their sexuality, then, was to be highly valued as a very specific and especially expressive sign of the covenant between God and his people. And if holiness for them was a matter of accepting the gift of each other's love wholeheartedly, then it would be a very incarnate kind of love in which the realities of sex played an important role.

To be sure, some would continue to see sexual abstinence as a stimulus to moral progress and a way of moving on further towards holy excellence. But more and more, sanctification would now be sought by married couples within the reality of their bodily and sexual lives. As a living sign of God's love, the married couple now was in quest of some spirituality that would not be a mere offshoot of monastic spirituality, that would be proper to their state of life. The periodical *L'Anneau d'or* and its guiding spirit, Abbé H. Caffarel, played an important role in this revitalization on conjugal and family prayer, in the family retreats and the sharing of spiritual experiences that were further promoted by the Equipes Notre-Dame.

But there is good reason to think that a larger movement was under way, of which the quest for a sounder marital spirituality was only a part. The search for a specifically lay spirituality would leave its impress on Christianity as a whole, not just on the married state. People were seeking to live their faith, their prayer life, and their sacraments in the very heart of the world and its manifold dimensions rather than in some isolated haven. At this point in time the search for a new equilibrium was a groping one. More disembodied currents of spirituality still persisted, though people criticized their roots in older and somewhat outdated perspectives. The persistence of these disembodied forms of spirituality was probably due in part to the fact that they were elaborated by clerics rather than rooted in marriage and family life.

Marriage and celibacy

Catholic Action had already helped to foster a new relationship between the priest and the laity. Family-circle groups would now have an even more decisive influence on priestly life. Numerous priests became actively involved in the family apostolate, mainly as chaplains to various family-circle groups. Many of them openly avowed that they were the ones to benefit the most from this new ministry.[12] Working with these family groups, priests were aware of receiving new insights and discovering important dimensions of human life. In particular, they came to glimpse a whole reality that was new to them: the life of the married couple and, through it, a feel for interpersonal relationships with all their affective and sexual components.

Those trained for the priesthood up to that time had, at best, a highly legalistic conception of marriage. Their attention had been focused on obligations and sins. In the seminary we had been told that confessional revelations about sex life and its deviations might well put our own celibacy to the test. Now it would be contact with happily married couples that would raise questions about our celibacy, though of course the lives of the couples were not without difficulties and trials.

Priests now began to engage in dialogue with generous-hearted families living a very incarnate form of life. They came to discover family life in a far more concrete and existential way, and to see the possibility of establishing friendship with all sorts of human beings—including women. This prompted some priests to reflect further on the meaning of celibacy itself. As yet there was no direct challenge to priestly celibacy. But contact with the family apostolate gave new urgency to the task of exploring its demands in a far more personal way.

The context would change as time went on, and in our day it is very different. But in that period the new positive evaluation of sexuality and the elaboration of a specifically conjugal spirituality helped many priests to make their own celibacy more deeply personal. They discovered its value, not only as a form of asceticism but as a way of consecrating themselves to God and being present to others. Lay people, for their part, also acquired a better understanding of the priest and his place in their lives. New, more functional relationships were established with him—less reverential, more centered around dialogue, more straightforward and fraternal.

Both lay people and priests felt the need to make clear the specific nature and character of their respective states in life: marriage on the one hand, celibacy consecrated to God on the other. Each state represented an indispensable form of security for those in it.[13] One of the more striking contributions was the book by Dietrich von Hildebrand which originally appeared in 1939 and which came out in a French edition in 1947; it discussed the basic issues of purity and virginity.[14]

Transmitting new insights to their offspring

Various groups and movements concerned with conjugal spirituality were not content with the notion of forming united, happy, and holy married couples. As they saw it, these couples in turn were to be centers radiating a good influence on the environment in which they lived. In committed dedication to the apostolate the married couple itself would truly find cohesion and fulfillment.

All agreed that the spirituality of the married couple should have its own peculiar role to play in the elaboration of a family spirituality. And the first beneficiaries of this revitalized conjugal life would be the children, of course. We now see the appearance of the first books designed to initiate children into the life and spirituality of the family: e.g., the series of books by Père Boigelot, who wrote under the pen name of Pierre Dufoyer. We also find many conferences being held to prepare people for marriage, these being sponsored both by youth groups and by adult groups.[15]

This concern to make one's children participants in a revitalized marital spirituality was both understandable and praiseworthy. For many couples, however, it would prove to be a source of great trial and suffering. I can recall the distress felt by dedicated couples of that day when they saw their adolescents drawing away from the practice of their religion. The parents had provided them with a truly adult example of religious practice, but one by one the children went their own way. The elaboration of a specifically conjugal spirituality had promised to usher in a new and decisive era in marriage and the Christian life. Now it became evident that it would not necessarily be passed on to the younger generation, not in any direct or tangible form at least. While the rich harvest of that marital renewal was incontestable, the succeeding generation would feel compelled to stand apart from it. It would make its own discoveries in its own different ways.

III. EXCESSES AND WIDER RAMIFICATIONS

Illusory yearnings for total fusion

Some couples would encounter trials and difficulties within their own little marital community, not so much because of the contemporary spiritual renewal itself but because of certain tendencies and exaggerations stressed by some.

The rediscovery of marital holiness and the quest for communion at every level awoke in some the illusory dream of total fusion. Books began to appear with titles that spoke of perfect love, total union, and complete harmony. The publication of Jacques Maillet's *Lettres à sa fiancée* had a profound impact on people. Some people now felt that the only important thing was to think alike, pray together, and do everything together. Nothing else mattered.

Sooner or later, however, people began to feel somewhat stifled in an atmosphere which left no room for the exercise of personal talents and the entertainment of individual yearnings. Instead of envisioning a community made up of communicative give and take between two different and autonomous human beings, some people had entered marriage with the notion that all distance between them would be eliminated for good.

This illusory ideal of total fusion would cause much impoverishment and dissatisfaction, and a reaction against it set it. There was, for example, the judicious article extolling imperfect marriage that was written by Robert

Bovet, a Swiss specialist on married life.[16]

Neglect of other lifestyles

All of this should suggest both the strengths and the weaknesses of those first stages in the rediscovery of married life and its spirituality. In those days it was common to find that married couples were deeply proud of their marital state, but it must also be said that this pride often went hand in hand with a disregard and even a disdain for other lifestyles and their possible worth.

The new Christian communities centered around marriage had a place for the priest-chaplain and for the member who lost his or her spouse. Other than that, however, most did not provide a place for widows, widowers, single people, or those in the religious life. Such traits of narrowness and limited vision, however, should not obscure the truly positive impact of this renewal. It made many homes more united, incarnate, and apostolic.

Impact on society and the Church

The developing movement of which we have been speaking here touched the intimate life of many couples. It is only to be expected that it would also begin to have an impact on surrounding society. Besides considering the evolving inner life of homes and families, we must realize the importance of analyzing the changes going on with regard to cultural models and the collective societal context. Thus, for example, we note a widespread eroticizing of societal life as a whole. Some groups, actively championing moral decency and propriety, reacted against this trend with promptness and courage—though perhaps not too judiciously. They made a serious effort to ensure that sexuality, which had been cloaked in silence and confined to the interpersonal level until a short time ago, would not now become a byword in societal discourse and life. And they were even willing to go to court to keep it out of advertising, films, magazines, and other media. This example itself should make it clear that the situation which we feel so keenly today was already in existence twenty or thirty years ago.[17]

Insofar as church life is concerned, the announcement of Vatican II and the preparations for it would excite great interest among those Christians involved in the renewal of marital and family life. Here was a chance to get the Church to recognize and formally endorse the transformations which they had come to perceive and live ever more fully in the last few decades. Here was a chance to break some of the impasses that still blocked the way: the older teaching on the primary end of marriage, the thorny issue of birth control, the legislation still governing mixed marriages, and the prohibitions regarding divorce which were regarded as too strict and intransigent by some.

More basically still, many priests and lay people involved in family movements felt that the time had come for the whole Church to benefit from the important discoveries and achievements of marriage renewal and revitalized conjugal life. And so a welter of data and material was collected and forwarded to the various commissions entrusted with the task of preparing Vatican II. But that marks the beginning of a new era which does not fall within the scope of this article.

Translated by John J. Drury

Notes

1. A.M. Carré, O.P., *Compagnons d'éternité. Le sacrement de mariage* (Collection Chrétienté, Paris: Ed. Du Cerf, 1938); A. Christian, *Ce sacrement est grand. Témoignage d'un foyer chrétien* (Paris: Association du mariage chrétien, 1938).
2. H. Doms, *Du sens et de la fin du mariage* (Paris-Bruges: Desclée de Brouwer, 1927).
3. Among the things which might seem shocking in *Casti connubii* to today's reader is its drastic evaluation of new currents of thought. Those currents, it claimed, threatened the very foundations of family life; and the only true guardian of family life was the Catholic Church. Over against this line of thought, however, we find passages which extol the life of the Christian family; it is the latter strain which many found to be stimulating in a positive sense.
4. The encyclical *Casti connubii* does discuss such issues in the traditional terminology of 'secondary ends'. Mutual aid and reciprocal lovemaking as a remedy for concupiscence are not forbidden so long as the intrinsic nature of the marital sex act is safeguarded and such secondary ends are kept subordinate to the primary end of marriage. Alongside this traditional strain, however, there are other passages in *Casti connubii* which had a profound impact on marriage renewal and which were used by theologians subsequently as support for a higher evaluation of conjugal love and its place within marriage. See, for example, Louis Lochet, "Les fins du mariage," in *Nouvelle Revue Théologique*, May 1951, pp. 449-465, and June 1951, pp. 561-586.
5. Paul Chanson, *Art d'aimer et continence conjugale* (Paris: Editions Familiales de France, 1949). The postscript (pp. 131-158) by Père H.M. Feret is entitled, "Art d'aimer et vie spirituelle chretiénne."
6. In March 1950, the imprimatur granted by the Archbishop of Paris was revoked. On 12 August 1950 two books by Paul Chanson were taken out of circulation, and explicit reference was made to the postscript by Feret. On 30 June 1952, the Holy Office issued its monitum.
7. For example, there was the favorable evaluation given by Père Rene Carpentier in the *Nouvelle Revue Théologique* (May 1950, pp. 546-548). See also his carefully worded commentary on the monitum of the Holy Office in the *Nouvelle Revue Théologique* (November 1952, pp. 974-980).

8. See, for example, Claude Servies, *La chair et la grâce* (Spes, 1948); Jacqueline Martin, *Plénitude, Témoignage d'une femme sur l'amour* (Editions Familiales de France, 1951); Dr. Jouvenroux, *Témoignage sur l'amour humain* (Editions Ouvrières, 1944).

9. Among the more outstanding articles and books we might mention several works by Jacques Leclercq: "Changements de perspective en morale conjugale," three articles in *Le prêtre et la famille* (1950), a publication put out by the Association du mariage chrétien; *Limitation des naissances et conscience chrétienne*, a work of joint authorship under the editorial direction of Henry Dumery (Paris: Editions Familiales de France, 1950).

10. Address of Pius XII to participants attending the convention of the Catholic Union of Italian Midwives (29-30 October 1951).

11. Henry Dumery, "Simples réflexions sur la méthode Ogino. A tous les époux qui s'interrogent devant la vie," in *Nouvelle Revue Théologique*, June 1948, pp. 587-597. This article was reprinted in *Limitation des naissances et conscience chrétienne*, pp. 251-263. That anthology also contains an excellent study by B. Besse, H. Dumery, and A. Laudrin (pp. 269-287).

12. Some periodicals which arose at this time were addressed specifically to priests: e.g., *Le Prêtre et la Famille*, published by the Association du mariage chrétien (France); and the *Notes de Pastorale Familiale*, a supplement to *Feuilles Familiales* that was for priests specifically (Belgium).

13. Simultaneously we find serious disdain and devaluation of any sort of celibacy not justified by some state of religious consecration. This vaunted pride in the married state and sacred celibacy probably served as a cover for unconscious feelings of insecurity.

14. Dietrich von Hildebrand, French edition, *Pureté et Virginié* (Paris: Desclée de Brouwer, 1947). There were many works which dealt with sacred celibacy and the relationship between marriage and celibacy: e.g., Marc Oraison, *Vie chrétienne et Problèmes de la sexualité* (Paris: Centre d'Etudes Laënnec-Lethielleux, 1952); R.P. Tesson, "Sexualité, morale et mystique," in *Mystique et Continence* (Les Etudes Carmelitaines, Desclée de Brouwer, 1952), pp. 357-379; J.M. Perrin, O.P., *La Virginité* (Cahiers de la Vie Spirituelle, Paris: Ed. du Cerf, 1952); Bishop Ancel, "Vocation religieuse et vocation au mariage," in *Pastorale Familiale* (Rennes: Congrès de l'Union des Oeuvres, 1949), pp. 285-302; Pierre de Locht, "Le célibat des prêtres," in *Le Prêtre et la Famille*, November-December 1952, pp. 1-10, and January-February 1953, pp. 1-6, with bibliographical references to the literature of the period. Although it extends slightly beyond the period covered in this present article, the following item is pertinent because it is the result of research undertaken in the years immediately preceding Vatican II: J.M. Pohier, "La Chasteté sacerdotale," in *Supplément de la Vie Spirituelle*, 1962, pp. 408-439.

15. In 1936 the Association du mariage chrétien published a collaborative effort entitled *La vie nous appelle: Vocation familiale et préparation au mariage*. It had already put out several works of this sort: *Pour bien élever vos enfants; L'Eglise et l'Education sexuelle;* and *Comment marier chrétiennement nos enfants?*

16. R. Bovet, "Eloge du mariage imparfait," in *L'Anneau d'Or*, Nov.-Dec. 1951, pp. 409-413: it summarizes an earlier conference published in German, *Lob der unvollkomen Ehe* (Zurich: Zwingli Verlag, 1951). In 1964 Théodore Bovet founded the periodical *Ehe: Zentralblatt für Ehe- und Familienkunde*; he had already written, among other works, *Das Geheimnis ist gross* (Berne: Ed. Paul Haupt), translated into French as *Le mariage, ce grand mystère* (Neuchâtel: Ed. Delachaux et Niestlé).

17. In preparing this paper I was astonished to read the first sentence of an article I wrote in 1953 for *La Revue Nouvelle* (15 February 1953): "No one can deny the fact that there is at present an abundance of publications of all sorts dealing with marriage, conjugal life, and sexuality. It is almost disgusting to see all that is being read and sold and displayed on the shelves of bookstores and newsstands."

Kajetan Kriech

A Firsthand Report on the Current Crisis In Catholic Sexual Morality

IT takes only the most cursory look at Catholic circles today for someone to realize that Catholic sexual morality is in a state of crisis. On the one hand some people are trying to overcome the crisis by formulating new ethical principles. Other people, however, are afraid that the least questioning of older norms and values will open the door wide to sexual promiscuity.

The following report will try to present this crisis in the most concrete terms possible.[1] It focuses only on the situation in Catholic circles within Switzerland. It should be of more general interest, however, because outside contacts indicate that the situation in other European countries does not differ essentially from that in Switzerland.

I. GENERAL TRENDS

The current trends can be summed up under two basic headings. People are calling for *a positive evaluation of sexuality* and for *a sexual morality based on personal responsibility*. Let us consider these two points.

A positive evaluation of sexuality

Letters sent to the Swiss bishops at the time of their 1972 Synod testify to a widespread feeling that "in the teaching of the Catholic Church sexuality is and has been consistently looked down upon as something bad," that "the sexual morality preached by the Church has always been far too negative." Young people in particular are expressing their opposition to the antisexual morality proposed by the Church: "The Church has consistently divided up human beings into two components: body and soul. It sees the body as something evil, the soul as something good. . . . Today we cannot accept that conception of human sexuality. It offers us no help at all when we try to come to terms with our sexuality in real-life practice. On the contrary, the heavy stress placed on the sixth commandment has often produced undeserved guilt feelings and complexes in young people, with fateful consequences for their later development."[2] The demand is put forward that the Church preach "a life-affirming sexual morality," utter a convincing and unconditional 'yes' in favor of human sexuality at every opportunity, and honestly own up to the "mistakes and flaws in her sexual ethics." She can regain her credibility only if she moves "from her former prudishness, and gets beyond the current sex-wave to a healthy sense of sex and sexuality."

However, there is no lack of opposing voices. Some point out that the present disorder in the sexual realm cannot be blamed on the Church, and that it is not the fault of earlier generations. In their view it is "a question of inner order and control." Others see the excessive emphasis on sex in the media and the public domain as the cause for the prevailing immorality and the current breakdown of marriage. It is here that the Church has an obligation to draw a clear distinction between proper and improper conduct in matters of sex, to tell people what exactly "is sinful, and what is not." While the other side seems to put too positive an evaluation on human sexuality, this side stresses the fallen aspect of human nature and its repercussions in the realm of sex. It also stresses the need for renunciation, moderation, and self-sacrifice as values associated with the following of Christ: "Without these dimensions associated with the cross, sexuality is devoid of any Christian foundation."

A sexual morality based on personal responsibility

The same demand crops up like a refrain in the letters sent to the Swiss bishops: the Church ought to get beyond a morality of mere commands and prohibitions; she ought to guide people towards an authentic sense of personal responsibility. Various reasons are put forth to justify this rejection of a morality based solely on precept and prohibition. Some point to the *societal upheaval* of the present day, in which the old transmitted moral principles and values "are being called into question more and more." In such a situation a "straight-jacket morality," a morality of "Thou shalt not," simply will not do. While such a morality might have been okay in a earlier day, it is merely an appendage in people's lives today. Since it does not really go to the core of the human person, it will crumble or fall off when the first storm of life hits it, "leaving only perplexity and despair in its wake."

Some want to be released from the patronizing tutelage of the Church and to be entrusted with a real sense of personal responsibility. They ask: "Does the Church really believe that every human being has been endowed with reason by God? Does the Church really take the sacrament of Confirmation seriously? One might well doubt it when one finds that in the Church all questions about sex, marriage, and family life are defined and regulated by unmarried people." In one letter the official church and the magisterium are compared to a traffic cop: "He signals directions, but he is not heeded because the traffic flows more smoothly without his intervention."

Some feel that church authorities have suffered a great loss in credibility by formulating laws and precepts without taking due note of the current findings of the human sciences. One cannot help but assume from the very start "that a large percentage of the faithful are not going to abide by those precepts." Others raise the more basic question as to whether and to what extent the whole issue of sexuality falls within the proper competence of the Church, and how it is related to faith at all. They feel that the answer to this question is of central importance.

The Synod's special interdiocesan Commission 6, hereafter referred to as Synod Commission 6, took up this question and reached the following conclusions. It said that the Church certainly does have the duty of expressing its view of sexuality on the basis of the Christian image of man. But this does not mean, it pointed out, that the Church should or could provide ready-made answers to the concrete questions of sexuality on the basis of the Christian image of man alone. In such matters she must always have recourse to the independent contributions which can be offered by pertinent disciplines and to the concrete lessons to be learned from living experience.[3]

Finally, people reject a morality of mere commandments and prohibitions by appealing to "an ethics deeply imbued with the spirit of Christ." What is needed is a whole new awareness. An ethics truly inspired by the gospel message could not possibly be content with mere commands and prohibitions. It would point up the positive values of human sexuality; orient human life around Christ, his teaching, and his life of love; work out solid supporting motives; and help people to form a sound conscience. Such an ethics would "take in the whole human being in all its facets and derive from an inner sense of personal responsibility rather than from something akin to a compulsive neurosis." Only such an ethics and approach could hold its own in the concrete situations that crop up in our rapidly changing times.

Here again, however, we find dissenting voices and people opposed to the idea of a morality based on personal responsibility. The staunchest opponents are those who rule out any possibility of compromise or agreement between "traditional Catholic teaching" and the "new morality." One is error, the other is truth; and "error can never serve as a real basis for discussion." Others are willing to admit that the desire for a morality of personal responsibility is justified, but they see great danger in it insofar as the lack of objective commandments and prohibitions would open the door to subjectivism. Still others feel that a real sense of responsibility presupposes personal maturity. That is comparably more difficult today than yesterday, when one "could hold on to firmly entrenched moral principles without having to think too much about it."

II. TWO FOCAL POINTS OF THE CRISIS

There is hardly any area of Catholic sexual morality that is not somehow affected by the present crisis, not even to mention the whole problem of sex education. Some are calling for a different evaluation and judgment of adolescent masturbation. As a phenomenon associated with a transitional stage of development, it might well not be a problem at all, and it could be judged accordingly. Meanwhile unmarried people are waiting for Catholic morality to take due account of their problems and difficulties in the realm of sex, and to stop making flat judgments about sexual relationships between single people. Insofar as homosexuality is concerned, people want Catholic morality finally to take cognizance of human beings who are more inclined towards people of their own sex. Like heterosexuals, they too can live their sexuality as a "gesture of love," and should not be ostracized by society.

But the present crisis seems to focus most pointedly on two particular issues: family planning and premarital sex. It is these two issues that we shall discuss in detail in the following pages.

Family planning

Many letters to the Swiss bishops express the view that Paul VI's encyclical *Humanae vitae* (hereafter cited as HV) was decisive in bringing the whole issue of responsible birth control to the very center of discussion and debate within the Church. Many correspondents openly express their *disappointment* with the papal encyclical, indicating that this is a generalized feeling among large numbers of Catholic married people. They had looked to Rome "with high hopes and full confidence," but the encyclical was "a slap in the face" and "a serious mistake." It "made no contribution whatsoever towards the solution of the problem of birth control." As some put it: "It would have been better for the Church not to have taken any stand at all on the matter of family planning than to have taken one which the overwhelming majority of the faithful view as anachronistic and incomprehensible."

Some express the view that the Church is "not competent" to speak on marital problems or to intervene in this area. As they see it, HV was a "tragic overstepping of the proper limits of church competence, for which there is not the slightest support in the Bible." It would have been far better and more correct for the Church "to leave the whole problem of the pill to science and to concentrate on educating the consciences of the faithful." The problem of birth control cannot be solved primarily by resorting to theoretical or theological viewpoints. One must look to reality in this matter: "The Ogino-Knaus approach (i.e., the rhythm method) cannot be relied upon"; "Restricting intercourse to infertile periods jeopardizes the marriage"; "Please realize the fact that the Ogino-Knaus approach simply cannot be used by many women."

Some letters zero in on the arguments of the encyclical and point out that they are not conclusive. They call for a complete reconsideration of the antinomy between 'natural versus unnatural', insisting that more weight must be given to the findings of the modern sciences (medicine in particular). As one letter-writer puts it: "Which is really more important, the personal sphere or the biological sphere? In my opinion, the personal sphere. But with its one-sided stress on infertile periods the papal encyclical makes it only too clear that the personal sphere is still subordinated to a purely biological and metaphysical overview."

Others would still be open to pastoral help from the official magisterium, but they feel that it should not try to go into details; the final decision should be left to *the conscience of the married couple.* Why? Because in this area one cannot formulate "a single recipe for all human beings"; "circumstances differ greatly from couple to couple." But the more basic reason is that "the conscience of each individual must ultimately decide such matters." Married people "are adult Christians with a real sense of personal responsibility. . . . The era of unconditional obedience and submissiveness is over."

Many letters express concern that in this area the Church may have unnecessarily overextended her authority. One pastor of souls remarks: "At the present moment in church history, it seems to me, the issue goes far beyond the single question of responsible birth control. It concerns the Church herself. The issue is the salvaging of her authority, the practice of authentic Christian obedience to that authority, and ultimately the *very credibility of the Church herself.*"

Humanae vitae contributed nothing to the solution of the burning issue. A large number of Catholics, therefore, have felt compelled to work out a solution without the help of the magisterium or in direct opposition to its views. It is true that episcopal conferences in different countries have tried to speak out on HV, and to offer pastoral help and suggestions that might contribute to a solution of the problem. But the real conflict remains: "On one side we have the prohibition of the Pope, whose thinking seems to be very one-sided on this matter. On the other side we have the views expressed by various episcopal conferences, which seem to mitigate the papal position. So where do we really stand now?"

People are quietly moving away from the Church, if not out of the Church. This "emigration" is growing in strength, and it is being reinforced rather than diminished by the positions taken by the bishops around the world. People can readily understand the concern of bishops to help people understand the Pope's position and respect his authority. But they cannot understand why the bishops seem to lack apostolic forthrightness and sincerity, why they are evading the whole question of truth and doing acrobatics with moral theology in order to help the faithful with this critical issue of conscience. One letter sums up the feeling with a request: "Please take a clearcut stand on the matter of birth control and stop hedging, so that the average person can understand what is what without having to resort to scholarly dissertations."

It is surprising to find how few letters to the Swiss bishops support HV unreservedly. Only an isolated letter here and there expresses *full agreement* with the views of the papal encyclical. One medical doctor writes that he has collected data from his own practice that strongly corroborates HV from a medical standpoint. Most of those who defend HV however, base their support on the contention that "morality and ethics might collapse" if it were not for the encyclical and its views. The opposition to HV is seen to be "the result of egotism." Without HV, "young people would give way completely to free love." The Church herself would suffer great harm if "she approved everything and let people do exactly what they felt like doing." When we are talking about something as great and important as our faith, "can we not expect people to make sacrifices?"

The views and opinions described so far are based mainly on the letters which lay people sent to the 1972 Synod of Swiss bishops. It is difficult to determine to what extent they reflect the views of the vast majority of Swiss Catholics. However, we get some additional data from a research poll conducted by the Zurich Institute for Research into Marriage and Family

Life. This particular poll was taken in the diocese of Chur during 1969 and 1970.[4] Since HV had come out a short time before and aroused much debate, the section of the poll dealing with marriage morality focused on issues brought up by the encyclical. Both Catholic married people and pastors were interviewed.

In their responses, *pastors of souls* indicated that an overwhelming majority of their faithful had a negative reaction to the papal encyclical.[5] Only 17.6% of the responding clergymen felt that the reaction of their parishioners to HV was predominantly positive. Insofar as the younger generation was concerned, only 10% felt that their reaction was predominantly positive.

In the opinion of pastors, it was they themselves who suffered the most from the publication of the encyclical; 39.6% felt this way. This datum is all the more impressive because here the clergymen were expressing their own personal experience, whereas the other responses were based merely on observation. 32.8% felt that the encyclical created difficulties mainly for young married couples. 32% felt it created most difficulty for couples around the age of forty.[6] On the basis of their pastoral experience, they felt that the encyclical caused no great difficulty for couples around the age of fifty; only 4% of the pastors disagreed with this statement. In all likelihood this is due to the fact that the practical problems of birth control are no longer a critical issue for this age-group.

When *married couples* were polled on the issue of birth control, their responses came out as follows:

— 9% of the responding couples felt they could manage without using an active method of birth control.
— 10% shared the view that the pill helped to foster the breakdown of marriage and outright divorce; this view, of course, was expressed often during debate on this issue.
— An astonishingly large percentage, however, were of the opinion that the choice of birth control method was up to the couple (78% total; urban 83%, industrial 78%, rural 70%). And 36.6% felt that the Church had put too much stress on the question of method.[7]
— A very small percentage (6.2%) expressed full and complete agreement with everything that *Humanae vitae* said. 5.9% agreed with this controversial statement in the encyclical: "Every marital act must remain open to the transmission of life." 27.6% were not sure whether that statement was correct or incorrect.[8]

On 11 December 1968, the Swiss bishops published a statement which sought to provide the faithful with some help and enlightenment regarding HV. In the poll of married people it turned out that almost half of them (46%) were unaware of the statement put out by the bishops. In all likelihood the reason was that radio, television, and the other media had not given the statement much coverage. 14.2% of the married respondents found the episcopal statement helpful; 5% thought it went too far; and 23.1% felt that it evaded all the "real questions."[9]

Premarital sex

A second major issue in the current crisis of Catholic sexual morality has to do with premarital sex. The poll taken in the diocese of Chur asked pastors and married people about this issue.

When pastors were asked about *the frequency of premarital sex* among young people, their responses were as follows:

— 39.1% felt that premarital sex was frequent; 9.0% felt it was almost the general rule. 13.9% felt that it was rare. 31.2% said they did not know how frequent it was.[10]

When married couples were asked about the frequency of premarital sex, their responses were as follows:

— 24.3% felt it was the general rule; 31.3% felt it was frequent; only 1% thought it was rare; and 25% said they did not know.[11]

When pastors were asked *how they judge premarital sex,* how they react to it pastorally when confronted with a case, they responded as follows:

— "Warn against it in general and on principle": 57.7% (urban 38%, industrial 65%, rural 70%);
— "Judge on the basis of a given case" (the basic distinction being before or after a formal engagement): 45.0% — urban 68%, industrial 31%, rural 25%;
— "Let it pass": 1% (urban 0%, industrial 3%, rural 0%);

On the whole, then the vast majority of pastors "warn against it in general and on principle." But a strong percentage (45.0%) are willing to "judge on the basis of a given case." A higher percentage of young clergymen are to be found in this category.[12]

When married couples were asked how they judge premarital sex, they responded as follows:

— "Up to the conscience of the parties involved": 55.3%;
— "See no objection to it if there is a serious intent to get married": 37.0%;
— "Useful for determining two people's compatibility": 15%;
— "Always justifiable": 6.2%;
— "Always a sin": 10.7%.[13]

Comparing the responses of clergymen and married couples on this point, we see that the former are much more likely to condemn premarital sex.

What about young people? What do they think of premarital sex? A married couple, members of the aforementioned Synod Commission 6, conducted an inquiry among young people in the French-speaking cantons of Switzerland. This question was included in their poll, and 1,640 young people responded.[14]

One question was: "Are young people in favor of trial marriages?" The responses given were: Yes, 24.63% (Catholics 23.50%; Protestants 27.63%); No, 52.7% (Catholics 53.06%; Protestants 46.71%).[15]

A second question was: "Are young people in favor of premarital sex?" The responses given were: Yes, 53.4% (Catholics 51.65%; Protestants 56.57%); No, 21.03% (Catholics 21.81%; Protestants 17.76%).[16]

The reason why a majority of young people are in favor of premarital sex is not readily clear from this poll. But we notice that a corresponding proportion of them are opposed to trial marriages. This might permit us to conclude that they tend to favor premarital sex when the assumption is that it will lead to an enduring bond between the two parties, but not when it is merely an experiment.

A group of young people from Baden formulated their views for the Synod as follows: "When someone is in love, it is only natural to express this love to the fullest and utmost, including sexual intercourse. In interpersonal relationships you cannot make a neat division between the bodily components and the spiritual components, and then isolate them from one another. The signs and tokens of love are manifold, leading step by step from kissing and petting to sexual intercourse. When two human beings reach a point in their relationship where they would like to express their spiritual and psychic closeness through the ultimate act of physical union, then they are faced anew with deciding whether they can do that in a morally responsible way. Suppose, however, that what had once been a dynamic relationship between them comes to a sudden halt because sexual intercourse is forbidden. They must then sacrifice the dynamic, ongoing quality of their relationship and plunge right into marriage. It thus becomes very difficult to deepen their own relationship. In such a case we see no moral objection to sexual intercourse because it is clearly an integral part of their mutual personal love."[17]

This viewpoint of some young people runs into strong opposition in certain circles. It is worth noting that the letters addressed to the 1972 Synod rarely touch directly upon the question of premarital sex; but where they do, most of the comments strongly warn against it. Here is one sample comment: "How often it happens that a person 'swears' fidelity in some relationship, only to run into someone else who seems more compatible and with whom he or she proceeds to have intercourse. The same thing can happen later in marriage. Such a person has never learned to control his urges. He surrenders unreservedly to instinctual impulses and calls that 'love'. The resultant marriage conflicts are known to every divorce court and marriage counsellor."

Others rely on psychology, sociology, and theology to show that the utmost caution and circumspection is called for: "In the last analysis no one, not even one's partner, can tell from the outside whether the act of intercourse is really an expression of personal love and relationship or not. All too often it is a cover for sheer egotism and cheap instinctual satisfaction."

Still others want "hard and fast norms," lest needed barriers and restraints give way altogether. In this area "the Church should have the courage to be old-fashioned. . . . Premarital restraint and continence should be restored as the proper attitude." If two people find that their interpersonal relationship has reached the point where they wish to express their love in the act of intercourse, then they should get married.

The young people from Baden, however, counter this latter point of view with a question of their own: "What, then, is marriage after all? Doesn't marriage really begin when two people are one in their own eyes and before the eyes of God? We believe that the Church makes marriage too dependent on the formal rite. It seems to us that marriage is not a value which is suddenly found at the 'marriage altar'. If the Church chooses to stress the sacramental value of marriage, we should like to point out that the spouses themselves are the ministers of this sacrament. In this connection the Church also seems to have forgotten that marriage cannot suddenly be there all at once. On the contrary, it is a dynamic reality involving a process of development and growth."[18]

Since we have tackled the issue of premarital sex in this report, we cannot fail to allude to the well-known 'Pfürtner case'. Pfürtner was ordinary professor of moral theology at the University of Freiburg. In November 1971 he presented a paper in Bern on the present crisis in morality, using the issue of sexual morality as his main example (*"Moral—was gilt heute noch? Das Beispiel der Sexualmoral"*). There was strong reaction to his paper in Switzerland and other countries. This led to his dismissal from his teaching post.

We cannot treat his theses in detail here, nor is that necessary.[19] The critical issues in the present crisis are brought out very clearly in the position paper issued by the Swiss episcopal conference on 14 March 1972: i.e., the tension between traditional church teaching and modern scientific research on the one hand, and between objective ethical norms and a morality based on personal responsibility on the other. Here is what the bishops have to say: "In judging premarital sex and masturbation the bishops are unanimous in adopting a clear and unmistakable position. It is their position that such behavior runs counter to objective ethical norms and the teaching of the Catholic Church which is still valid today. However, they would not rule out the necessity of judging the matter of subjective guilt and personal responsibility on a differential basis."[20] They also call upon all "to be objective in their discussions, to avoid mutual recrimination and general condemnations, and to be doers of truth in the matter of love."[21]

That concludes my firsthand report. It bears witness to a general atmosphere of anxious searching and personal uncertainty. We can no longer talk about a single unified view of sexual ethics being shared by all Catholics. That does not mean, of course, that certain basic values are not recognized by all. Nor does it mean that anyone is advocating sexual promiscuity. The majority of Catholics want more frankness and candor from the magisterial Church, and less detailed prescriptions. They also want more personal responsibility for the individual lay person. A small minority disagrees vehemently. In this time of upheaval they want clearcut guidelines and straightforward commands and prohibitions. Many unresolved problems remain to be worked out, some of them having to do with fundamental theology and some with moral theology.

Translated by John J. Drury

Notes

1. This report is based primarily on the following sources: (1) letters of Swiss Catholics to the 1972 Synod of Swiss bishops; (2) suggestions and proposals submitted to Synod Commission 6; (3) draft documents and other reports of the Synod; (4) polls and surveys taken in Switzerland concerning problems of sexual morality. The plethora of material and the limitations of this report compel me to concentrate on a few crucial issues.

2. "Was erwartet die Jugend von der Kirche bezüglich menschlicher Geschlechtlichkeit?" A draft document of Synod Commission 6, which was concerned with the issue of "marriage and family life in a changing society."

3. "Aktuelle Schwerpunkte zum Thema Sexualität," Diocesan Synod 6, No. 1.2.2.

4. "Situation und Bedürfnisse der Ehe- und Familienpastoral in der Diözese Chur: Arbeitsbericht—Ergegnisse—Folgerungen einer im Auftrag des Seelsorgerates durchgeführten Umfrage" (Zurich: Institut für Ehe- und Familienwissenschaft, 1970).

5. *Ibid.*, 93 f.

6. *Ibid.*, 95.

7. *Ibid.*, 156.

8. *Ibid.*, 158.

9. *Ibid.*, 163.

10. *Ibid.*, 76.

11. *Ibid.*, 132.

12. *Ibid.*, 78. "Warn against it in general and on principle": 37.5% of clergymen between the ages of 20 and 30; 63% of those over 70. "Judge on the basis of a given case": 79% of those between 20 and 30; 0% of those over 70.

13. *Ibid.*, 132.

14. "Des jeunes de Suisse romande s'expriment: Enquête réalisée auprès de jeunes romands de décembre 1971 à avril 1972," 1972 Synod, in manuscript form.

15. *Ibid.*, 46.

16. *Ibid.*, 48.

17. "Die Jungen und ihre Stellung zur Sexualität," in *Drehscheibe Synode 72*, 7 (July 1971, Zurich), No. 66.

18. *Ibid.*

19. For further discussion see K. Kriech, "Schwerpunkte in der moraltheologischer Diskussion um Pfürtners Vortrag in Bern," in *Schweiz. Kirchenzeitung*, 140 (1972): 141-145.

20. *Schweiz. Kirchenzeitung*, 140 (1972): 181.

21. *Ibid.*

Margareta Erber

Biological and Anthropological Data on Sexuality Disregarded by the Catholic Church

THE use of such terms as 'sexual activity' and 'sexuality' is very varied. Nevertheless we shall not begin with any definition. What should be brought out is that sexuality is not restricted to the genital zone, is not exhaustively covered under the notion of instinctual activity, and is not simply identified with the biological apparatus for procreation alone. Indeed biology itself can no longer stop with the procreative aspect of sexuality since ethology has taken shape as a distinctive discipline. The other point to be noted is that when we use the notion or concept of sexuality, something not objectifiable is always part of the picture.

The image which a human being has of his or her own sexuality, and of sexuality in general, is affected by his or her own knowledge and personal experience. The biologist has much to contribute to the description of sexuality. Biology provides that broad background of facts and data which brings human sexuality into sharp relief. This body of knowledge is not confined to the classic work of M. Hartmann on the sexuality of all living beings.[1] It includes, first and foremost, the findings of genetics, physiology, and ethology. It also includes the important findings of more recent research on the ontogenetic development and the hormonal basis of sexuality.

The biologist cannot throw this freight overboard, even when he or she may wish to do so on the basis of his or her own world view. For it gives objectivity to his or her image of sexuality.

When the biologist speaks specifically about the sexuality of human beings, then he is speaking as an anthropologist. I have attempted to spell out how anthropology today sees its role in this matter elsewhere.[2] The point I would like to make here is simply that we cannot talk about humans solely from the one-sided standpoint of a *single* science or discipline. Even the biologist must step outside his own scientific field if he wishes to integrate his biological findings. That is a legitimate procedure, not an unwarranted overstepping of the proper bounds. It is 'legitimate' precisely because the object itself determines what is right and correct. The real meaning and import of organismic relations surfaces in the ongoing history of personal self-development. Fairness is also demanded of the person who attempts to view the object in question. It would like the viewer to experience it as it really is. That is wisdom, according to Thomas Aquinas.

Insofar as sexuality is concerned, such wisdom does not seem to be very widespread in the Catholic Church at the present time. Is there a lack of willingness to pay heed to biological and anthropological findings? What have theologians and pastors of souls made of recent scientific developments? Many do indeed seem to have the feeling that their older conceptions have been stripped of their underlying foundation. But they do not seem to realize that what once was labelled 'Christian' no longer deserves that appellation. We cannot call something 'Christian', if it is shown to be inhuman. What is Christian should not do violence to what is human.

Apparently it is very difficult to draw the conclusions which flow from the basic underlying facts. Here, then, I should like to sketch the underlying bases and features of sexuality so that we may draw some of the attendant conclusions. However, I have given up the idea of going into any detailed description or of explaining the basic epistemological approach. There certainly would be room to go into *one* example in detail. But if I did that, I would have to give up the idea of touching upon all the varied starting points and the full range of biological data. Here, then, I shall sketch out some of the pertinent data. If the reader wishes to go into detailed biological explanations or presentations, there are plenty of books in the field.

The borderline nature of the approach used by someone who is coming to anthropology from *biology* stems from the fact that sexuality must be described both from the standpoint of living organisms in general and from the standpoint of *homo*. Not only do both have something to do with the same reality; in this particular case they coincide. The reality, in this instance, is called 'the body'. The person manifests itself as body. The bodily components are not neutral or indifferent, either with respect to the expressive content of one's outward appearance or with respect to one's way of reacting. It is Buytendijk who has gone deeply into the way that human beings present themselves, express themselves, communicate and live out their lives in bodily terms.[3]

Present-day anthropology also presents a picture of man's life and existence as a bodily entity. And since each body exists as one endowed with sex, sexuality is something more than a peculiar feature of humans. The integral wholeness of man prohibits us from regarding *homo* as an amalgam and describing humans as a 'being of nature' and a 'being of culture'. At best the latter notions are of some methodological use. In most cases, however, this formulation oversimplifies the matter far too much.

People try to combine two extreme standpoints. Some maintain that sexual behavior is biologically conditioned. Others, sociologists in particular, are of the opinion that man and his sexuality are the product of environment alone. In reality, however, it is not a matter of choosing between two alternatives or of simply combining inherited features with acquired features. The usual formulation does not really help to solve the question because the link between heredity and environment is really much more closely knit. The interplay between them evolves and develops as time goes on. Hence sexuality is a product of both prenatal and postnatal development.

Here I must bring up the findings of modern biology regarding the various processes of differentiation and its new insights into what is usually called 'determination'. All the observations and findings of biology indicate the following:

1. The 'nature' of man and his sexuality resides precisely in the fact that what is innate, including what is inherited, is constantly undergoing change. This changeability applies not only to human behavior but also to the physiological and anthropological bases of behavior.
2. Consequently the individuality of human beings and their sexuality is the most significant outcome of their evolution and development.

Obviously we must try to use and apply the new data and findings of the biological sciences. I shall start off, therefore, by considering human sexuality in the light of some basic features: (1) as a product of man's integral and bodily nature; (2) as a dynamic reality, even as man himself is; and (3) as marked by individuality, even as man himself is. Then I shall proceed to consider some of the data from more recent disciplines and the implications for sexual questions.

Sexuality in the light of man's integral and corporeal nature

Biological science provides anthropology with the basic and fundamental conception of *an integral Whole or totality.* If we accept that conception as our starting point, we have a basic criterion for any and all sex education. But any sex education based on such a criterion will frequently clash with the views and conceptions of the Catholic Church. Her present opinions and judgments about adolescent sexual behavior, for example, do not show any awareness of the fact that sexuality contributes to the overall development of personality. Instead of fostering and elaborating this insight, her pedagogical view is tainted with pessimism. The concrete practice and exercise of sexuality is rejected, for example. That is right enough, insofar as such exercise is superficially interpreted as a 'sampling' process. But on the other hand human beings must learn through experience that sense pleasure and happiness are dependent on the security and safety which comes from partnership.

The fact that in the enjoyment of sex human beings experience the feeling of being loved is grounded on their corporeality, on their bodily nature. Tenderness, then, must be learned. If we restrict sexuality to the genital zone, then the potential depths of sexual experience will never be plumbed. Because human beings are an integral Whole, precoital and coital activities form a continuum. Hence the guiding norm should be whether the various forms of childhood and adolescent sexuality lead the participants towards encountering each other as integral totalities. One case of petting, for example, can be very different from another. In one instance it may come down to mutual masturbation. In another instance, where it is part of love play in all its diversity, it may greatly enhance communication between the partners. So we must decisively reject any casuistry on this matter and completely rethink the notion of sin.

Consider the notion of purity for example. In many instances does it not come uncomfortably close to being equated with the notion of abstinence? And isn't impurity still defined in physiological terms? Church teaching and preaching must make it clear that purity or impurity becomes a reality within the framework of sexual activity. The institutional aspect alone cannot be normative in this area. Only when there is a partnership relationship involved, is it possible to establish rules and limits. When people's sexual lives do not go hand in hand with a solemn ceremony in church, the judgment of anthropologists about their sexual activity is bound to clash with that of canon lawyers.

Again and again appeals are made to the spirit and the will. They are to restrain people's sexuality, which is viewed negatively, instead of helping them to integrate it into a truly total and comprehensive love life. Yet if we could combine sound anthropological data with the authentic Christian goal of love, we could come up with a much deeper approach and presentation. It certainly would be more satisfactory than the principle of 'responsibility' or 'consideration' espoused by Alex Comfort.[4]

It is not just in passing judgment on adolescent sexuality that individual sex acts are isolated from the whole fabric of interconnected relationships. Whenever coitus itself is treated in isolation, we are going against the essential nature of human sexuality and the whole, integral relationship between the sexes. If the shared experience of mutual orgasm has any significance whatsoever, we simply cannot make coitus the one and only criterion of a 'consummated marriage'. We certainly cannot designate the insertion of the penis into the vagina as the determining factor. Yet those are the questions which still stand in the foreground of attention when the Church is considering the nullification of a marriage. No questions are asked about the personal aspects of the action: i.e., whether it was done to give pain or pleasure, whether it was done willingly or reluctantly, whether it was done with warmth and ardor or in a cold, dispassionate way, and so forth.

The same diminishing of sexuality underlies the counsel to live "as brother and sister." This may mean that the people involved are to avoid coitus, in which case sexuality is narrowly restricted and distorted. Or it may mean that the two people involved are to live a life without sexual activity. This runs directly counter to their partnership, for human sexuality is characterized by the fact that it is a medium of interpersonal communication. The same thesis can be deduced from ethological observations, as we shall see later on in this article.

The capacity for sexual experience is closely bound up with human existence as a whole. Yet this connection is not seen at all by many Catholics, just as it is not taken into consideration in many current sexual practices. Both standpoints fail to do justice to the place of sexuality in man's life as a Whole. For a corporeal human being sensual pleasure and orgasm, integrally united, are of such positive import that they must be approved wholeheartedly and without reservations. But instead of finding a positive appreciation of sexual excitability, pleasurable sensations, and sense gratification, we see that prejudices and cliches favoring sexual asceticism prevail. The latter is alleged to make extraordinary accomplishments and experiences possible. Rarely is it acknowledged that the stilling of basic needs is closely bound up with clairvoyant experiences, that such experiences are grounded in man's bodily nature as it is described in a biologically based anthropology. When sexual activity is devalued in biological terms, then church commentaries are akin to those of the libertine.

Though the linkup between sexuality and love cannot be proven on the grounds of natural science, it is not an unproven assertion. Awareness of this linkup springs from a comprehensive experience of reality. Even on the physiological plane, sexual activity is all the more complete and fulfilling when the harmony between the two parties involved is greater. It is also in the nature and character of human sexual life that loving union should possess an absolute and lasting quality. Pastoral and pedagogical disciplines are guilty of a great mistake when they do not help human beings to reach complete fulfillment in this respect. They should offer encouragement and help people to increase their capabilities in this area rather than concentrating on admonitions and prohibitions. The quality of integral wholeness and totality may be regarded sympathetically in Catholic circles, but unfortunately the Catholic Church has not drawn the attendant conclusions concerning the proper integration of sexuality into human life.

The dynamic and individual character of human sexuality

It is not surprising, then, that only grudging attention has been paid to the concept of *nature* worked out by modern biology. Of course the competence of biology in this area has not been denied, but little heed has been paid to its dynamic view of human nature and sexuality. There certainly can be no doubt that the encyclical *Humanae vitae* once again displayed the Church's penchant for an outdated concept of nature. It is not modern biology but *Humanae vitae* and its concept of nature that tries to pigeonhole man in a narrow biological schema akin to that of the isolated natural sciences.

What about the *individual* character of human sexuality? Perhaps more justice is done to this feature of human sexuality? Perhaps we are willing to move beyond the old and now outdated notions of heredity and determination and see human sexuality as the product of a complicated development in which many factors play a part?

Unfortunately it seems that there is little willingness to recognize the variety and variability of human sexual behavior. It is not just that no distinctions are made when it comes to judging the sexuality of people living celibate lives. Even when it comes to establishing norms for sexual behavior in partnership relations, no attention is paid to the individuality found there. And the official spokesmen of the Church are most unfair when it comes to any sort of sexuality that stands out as different or divergent: e.g., that of the homosexual. When the bishops of West Germany convened one of their general synods, one commission of experts tried to do some justice to the individual sexuality of the homosexual in a draft document dealing with "The Structure and Import of Human Sexuality" (July 1973). In discussing homosexuality, it did not once equate it with heterosexuality or put it on the same level. Yet in their official reaction, the bishops described this attempt to recognize sexual individuality as "intolerable."

More recent data and scientific findings must be taken into account, not only for the sake of truth but also because only in this way can we work out truly Christian patterns of conduct. Up until now, for example, we have not been able to provide homosexuals with a Christian line of conduct that will enable them to lead a meaningful life.

With the notion of 'individuality' we come to the uniqueness of each and every human being. The corresponding aggregate of features in him or her includes, among other things, the features specific to his or her sex. The latter enter into the whole interplay of individual features, but they are often overstressed. When we try to go back to the underlying reasons for this excessive emphasis on sex-specific features, we often come up with ideological motives.

'Motherliness', for example, is designated as a quality peculiar to females. From biological research we know that there is no such inherited characteristic. Among other animals we note an instinct to care for the young during the breeding period; we find something similar among human beings. The existence of a 'baby context' can contribute to the development of mothering behavior, for example. In any case this human instinct is not restricted to the female sex. Motherliness itself is not an instinct but a personal way of acting. The loving relationship to a child, which the term stands for, can and should be realized equally by the father.

Much the same holds true for the alleged inactivity of females in the sexual sphere. Both notions are closely bound up with the role accorded to women in human sexual life and society. While sex-specific patterns of behavior do result from the anatomical and physiological differences between men and women, these should not be confused with historically conditioned divisions of roles. The import of real sex differences for our sexual lives must be uncovered through careful scientific research. Some data on this issue is already available, but I shall not go into it here.

The actual status and condition of our sexuality at a given moment is bound up with our stage of growth and development. What we have achieved and put together for ourselves is of crucial importance. Whether we will attain the goal and purpose of sexuality depends on all that, not on momentary control over our sexual impulses and instinctual drives.

The relevance of ethology

To speak of the goal and purpose of sexuality is to bring in the whole question of its functions. And when we talk about giving shape and direction to our sexuality, we must have some solid knowledge about what is rather indiscriminately referred to as 'instinct'. Answers to both of these questions are provided by ethology, a more recent branch of biology. In its initial stage it was more concerned with comparative observations. Today it has broadened in scope to cover questions of a causal-analytical nature and to include measurement techniques within its methodology. Behavioral psychology, in particular, relies heavily on this discipline.

Phylogenetic processes and occurrences are the reason why the findings of ethology are relevant for *homo sapiens.* The novelty of the human species vis-à-vis other animals is to be found in systematic arrangements. We find elements in man that are also present in the rest of the animal kingdom; but in the human species they are systematically related to each other in ways that are not verified in the rest of the animal kingdom. The very first principle one learns from behavioral research is that behavior patterns and their individual components must always be considered as species-specific. In each species, in other words, they not only arise under different conditions but also have different duties to perform.

This methodological principle from ethology takes on particular significance when it is applied to the human species. On the one hand the basic disposition underlying human sexuality can be studied in all its purity in other animal species. On the other hand comparisons between species reveal the species-specific nature and distinctiveness of human sexuality.

In nonscientific circles, the relevance of the species-specific concept and its attendant relationships often goes unheeded. We hear vociferous critics of pornography talking about people who wallow in it like 'pigs'. This mistakenly suggests that man is simply an amalgam of animal and nonanimal components, and that he can somehow stop being human and react purely as a lower animal. Yet these same zealots will often propose the contrary view that it is not proper to compare human beings with brute animals.

Ethology runs up against this mistrust both in the Church and in society. Perhaps that is why the findings of this discipline have not had much of an impact, though they are fraught with consequences in many areas. Consider, for example, the *functions* of sexuality. Here is what H. Wickler has to say in summing up some of the interrelated data: "Outside the sphere of human nature sexual union (fertilization), procreation (preservation of the species), and pair-binding are different goals and values, each separable from the others and attainable in isolation. Likewise we find in the extrahuman sphere that a natural process leads to the point where more than one of these goals is attained through one and the same means. . . . Thus fertilization is linked up secondarily with procreation, and similarly sexual union is used to achieve pair-binding."[5]

The two connotations or meanings of copulation become particularly clear and obvious where nature separates them: "This occurs among the primates, among hamadryas baboons for example, where copulation also serves to establish a bond between the individuals."[6] Instead of describing other ways in which nature effects a separation between the sex act and procreation, I shall focus here on the effect of pair-binding between individuals.

Since we can establish that even among brute animals copulation serves to establish a perduring bond, the sex act can hardly play a lesser role in the human I-Thou relationship. Pairing appears on the scene as a distinctive value alongside that of procreation. And in the human species it attains a high level and rank indeed, which is immediately verifiable in concrete experience even though it can no longer be demonstrated by the natural sciences as such.

If people possess this experience, and if they also are aware of the relationships prevailing in the realm of living beings, they can hardly regard as reliable and competent the teaching of the Catholic Church that every marital act must remain open to the transmission of life. Such a view entails a misconception of sexuality. Nor does it consider the clear intrinsic value of human sexuality and draw the resultant conclusions with respect to premarital sex, the sexuality of older people, and the lifestyle of single people and celibates. Catholic pedagogy and pastoral activity is in danger of being restrictive and repressive rather than constructive. In the latter approach it sees a danger that the communicative power of sexuality and its value for personality development at every stage will be used up or exhausted. It does not see the danger in recommending a falsely conceived brand of sublimation and a type of control over one's impulses that is contraindicated by the underlying biological principles.

If the Church were open to some orientation in this matter, she could find guidelines for constructing a solid picture of sexuality in the biological sciences, particularly in the discipline of ethology. Whereas representatives of the Church still continue to hold the theory that depicts man as a flawed biological entity, that view was given up long ago in biology itself.

I had people cull statements from Catholic sources which spoke directly or indirectly about 'instinct' and 'instinctual life'. I could find no agreement whatsoever on the use of this concept. In most instances no attempt was made to work out a definition. Nowhere did the texts evince any familiarity with the findings of biology on this subject. But it is not enough to use the word 'instinct' as a shorthand term for a release of impulsive energy. Instinct must be studied as the embodiment or realization of a neural structure. Only then does one have in hand this particular motivation behind behavior.

Instinct, appetency, and external stimuli

Whereas psychology views instinctual drives or impulses from the standpoint of concrete experience, biology describes them from the standpoint of observation. Biology offers us knowledge about reflexes, about the possibility of canalizing and training them. Since the behavioral unity of highly complex instincts cannot be explained in terms of a stimulus-response model, there is a need to focus on such matters as appetency and its measurability, innate triggering mechanisms, the periodicity of their appearance, their typical course, and their goals—partial or otherwise. Particularly usable are the findings dealing with the interlacing of endogenous and learned movements and with the physiological bases of the elements enumerated above.

One may agree to whatever definition of 'instinct' one chooses. One may restrict the term to the appetency itself and the resultant search-behavior, or one may include the whole schema of instinctual functions in the definition. What is more important, however, is that one be acquainted with the individual factors involved and their interrelationship.

I cannot spell out all the consequences of this for praxis, so I shall let one example stand for many. To someone familiar with the relationship between appetency and external stimuli, the old counsels and educational measures designed to inculcate control over the instincts will seem either nonsensical or downright harmful. We simply cannot ignore the system of self-regulating mechanisms that we possess by inheritance. If serious study of the instinctual life is played down or mocked, the latter will take its own revenge. Closer attention to this subject, on the other hand, will bring us closer to the desired ethical goals.

We would do well to grasp the role of the biological component in motivating sexual activity, so that we may recognize its role in determining a given line of conduct. We do not get any further ahead by excluding that problem from consideration. The fact that we must go into this issue anyway should not be viewed and resolved so negatively as it was in the familiar old version of the 'double standard'.

Biological facts and findings help us to understand how we can correctly and successfully use our innate mechanisms, supplement them, and incorporate them into our lives. For example, we will link up the appetency-stimulus schema with the external stimulus involved. It makes a difference whether pornography or a partner is the stimulus for sexual arousal, whether the triggering factor is a personal or impersonal one. The stimulus-threshold also offers a starting point for considering impulse-formation.

The shaping of sexuality can also be approached from another direction of biological research: i.e., the analysis of man's heightened learning capacity that is based on the structure of the human brain. Here we can benefit from the insight that an acquired pattern of behavior can be linked up with an innate drive, and that an acquired stimulus can be linked up with an innate behavior pattern.

Conclusion

I have only been able to focus on a few of the many possible starting points in this attempt to show that the approach of biology offers us an opening into the whole problem of sexuality. For example, another possible starting point not considered here would be such basic biological phenomena as heterosexuality, bisexuality, and intersexuality. If human beings want to be able to understand their own nature, they must try to gain a better understanding of biology. Are the eyes of the Catholic Church closed to the relevance of the profane sciences?

Let me sum up three very relevant conclusions derived from biology:

1. It is not possible to derive human sexuality solely from organic processes. But it is up to physiology to shed light on the factors or mechanisms which facilitate or inhibit it.
2. Through a legitimate existential interpretation of the biological elements and findings, we can do away with unsatisfactory and misguided conceptions about sexuality. We can come to realize, in short, that all the anatomical and physiological factors not only have specific goals but also fashion a specific form of concrete life and existence.
3. Only a positive interpretation and evaluation of sexuality can do justice to this matter. The sexual pessimism of the Catholic Church cannot.

The lack of openness in the Catholic Church to biological and anthropological data is curious indeed. Is it preventing the faithful from living their sexuality in a truly human way?

Translated by John J. Drury

Notes

1. M. Hartmann, *Die Sexualität* (Stuttgart, 1956).
2. M. Erber, "Die Bedeutung der modernen Anthropologie in der Geschlechtererziehung der Schule," in *Naturwissenschaften im Unterricht*, Vol. 19 (1971), No. 5, p. 211.
3. F. Buytendijk, *Prolegomena einer anthropologischen Physiologie* (Salzburg, 1967).
4. A. Comfort, *Der aufgeklärte Eros* (Munich, 1966).
5. W. Wickler, "Das Missverständnis der Natur des ehelichen Aktes in der Moraltheologie," in *Stimmen der Zeit*, 1968, No. 11, p. 292.
6. H. Kummer, *Social Organization of Hamadryas Baboons* (Basel—New York, 1968).

Marie Augusta Neal

A Sociological Perspective on the Moral Issues of Sexuality Today

THE relation of sexuality to religious belief can be discussed meaningfully, it seems to me, only within the context of a religious commitment rooted in the gospel injunction to share God's creation with all the people. That context at the present time is the Church's commitment to the poor of the world.

As long as the central human need called for was continued motivation to propagate the race, it was essential that religious symbols idealize that process above all others. Given the vicissitudes of life in a hostile environment, women had to be encouraged to bear children and men to support them; child-bearing was central to the struggle for existence. Today, however, the size of the base population, together with knowledge already accumulated about artificial insemination, sperm banking, cloning, make more certain a peopled world. The more serious human problems are now who will live, who will die, and who will decide. The central fear and dread of our times is no longer that the human race might die out but that some people might face extermination for the sake of the others and these people are the poor of the world. In such a context, the pyramidal structure of decision-making systems, so long modeled on the patriarchal family with its tradition of father-right, is a source of grave anxiety to those with little or no power. At the same time, the fear of being overthrown by the organized masses stimulates those who have power to affirm whatever in the old tradition stands to legitimate their continued right to rule. Christianity, with its gospel message to serve the Lord by serving the oppressed, is caught within these forces. There is the double dread of an élite being served by the masses and total extinction which would result if the 'enemy' were to get control of the system.

Religious sacralization has always developed around what is feared and dreaded. We are witnessing today the de-sacralization of the patriarchal family as model for business firms, industry, government, educational systems and other organizations. Desacralization occurs whenever the unrepresented have learned that people who make decisions for others, who are not members of their interest group, make these decisions against the outsiders. Self-representation is part of the process of the development of peoples. Although in the past religion and science affirmed the sacredness and the naturalness of hierarchy and bureaucracy, today these things are called into question because of the exploitative uses to which they have been pressed by the elite in government and industry. Today father-right has been replaced by human rights as the ethical norm for international relations as well as for communal relations under the law. Even though the Catholic Church and the World Council of Churches have affirmed the declaration of these human rights in the United Nations Charter, only now are the fuller implications of their affirmation becoming manifest, as the poor rise up to claim what is rightfully theirs. The affirmation of human rights makes of equal importance, the availability of opportunities for men and women, whites and non-whites. It provides a new ethic and brings into question long-established white male ascendancy. It affects sexual relations as well as racial relations. In various parts of the world, non-white people and women of all colours are becoming conscious of the assumptions of their inferiority, assumptions systematically enforced through social conditioning in order to provide a legitimization for their relegation to servile tasks in the interest of the dominant males. Women are searching for ways in which to correct inhuman presuppositions about inferiority and superiority. History is correcting such errors, as people raise to consciousness the tacit assumptions embedded in centuries-old educative materials and other forms of indoctrination. Oppressed peoples demand civil rights and respect; and now women are demanding, beyond these, further knowledge of and control over their own bodies. The way these various factors relate to one another is still obscure to those immersed in a long tradition of the exploitation of persons. Moreover, art and religion frequently compound this obscurity, functioning to refine ambiguities and render them respectable.

The new concern for human rights arises out of the experience and knowledge of the two-thirds of the world that lives below the level of subsistence, despite the fact that we have the technological potential to provide the health, education and welfare services to remedy that problem. What we lack are the social relations needed to produce and distribute durable goods effectively for human use and to re-allocate resources on the basis of human need. The growing consciousness among the poor peoples of the world of their right to participate in the decisions that affect their lives, and to develop the resources of the places where they live rather than to have those resources used in the interest of multi-national corporations and the powerful nations of the world, has stimulated the Catholic Church and the World Council of Churches to affirm those rights and to support in the context of the gospel this movement toward a more human world (Pope John, 1963; *Gaudium et Spes*, # 26; Pope Paul, 1967). It is that movement that stimulated the re-ordering of priorities for the structure of the Church, that was evident in the Second Vatican Council's *Dogmatic Constitution on the Church*, in which the community of the people of God is accorded a priority over the juridical, hierarchical structure designed to minister to its needs (*Lumen Gentium*, chapters II and III). We have only begun to realize the implications of the changing structure of our Church. Founded to be a community of peers, all sons and daughters of the same Father, we are beginning to feel the demand for a new symbol of unity; a symbol that is circular and not pyramidal; a symbol that does not associate expressive and instrumental skills but combines them in single units. In the Church today human community needs to be celebrated with all the pomp and ceremony with which father-right has been celebrated in the past. Even to return to the Scripture to find its meaning for our times, new symbols and a new language need to be developed. Theologies are needed which can articulate this new life that is struggling to be recognized as the Church. It is a life predicated, not on the rule of elites over masses in the image of fathers over children, but on the development of human beings.

The theologies of liberation developing around the issues of oppression in Latin America provide the context for the emergence of new gender-relations between men and women, relations that do not rest primarily on biological differences associated with the bearing of children. Even those theologies, sensitive as they are to the oppression of poor peoples, are not yet couched in language sensitive to the oppression of women (Gutierrez; Segundo). Juan Luis Segundo's theological method — based on what he calls a hermeneutical circle — provides a way of approaching that problem. The circle begins with our way of experiencing reality, an experience which gives rise to ideological suspicion. This suspicion, of ideological superstructures in general and of theology in particular, is followed by a new way of experiencing theological reality, an experience which in turn gives rise to a theological suspicion about our customary hermeneutics. This leads to a new way of doing hermeneutics which appeals for a new human reality, thus beginning the whole process anew. Applied to the experience of women's status since the Council, this sequence puts the examinations of the issue of sexuality into an entirely new context.

John L. McKenzie describing the Roman Catholic Church in 1969 and Martin Marty, Protestantism in 1974, sense this new context (McKenzie, pp. 268-269; Marty, p. 322).

The end of the era is forewarned and directed by Pope Paul when, in *The Development of Peoples* and again in *The Eightieth Year Letter* on the anniversary of *Rerum Novarum*, he called Christians to action and urged the laity to transform structures 'without waiting passively for orders and directives, to take the initiative freely and to infuse a Christian spirit into the mentality, customs, laws and structures of the community in which they live'. All this was said in the context of action for the elimination of injustices (Pope Paul, 1971, # 48). The injustices specifically referred to were the usurpation of the world's resources by one-third of the world, to the exploitation of the other two-thirds. The right to life of living peoples is systematically denied to two-thirds of the people in social systems in which crumbs from the master's table are awarded in paternalistic fashion to the desperately poor, while the industrial producers and their benefactors deliberate on how they will accord assistance to the poor in future disasters. That part of the Church which is caught up in such a system is currently being addressed by another part, a part that has been freed from this structure by meditating on the gospel in company with the poor and by the mandate of the *Pastoral Constitution on the Church in the Modern World* to work with the poor for their own liberation. The dynamic of this confrontation provides the context in which issues of sexuality need to be addressed.

What sociology teaches about sexuality is that the ethic the Church has continued to reinforce was the common ethic of Western society prior to the development of an enormous population base. Even in 1969 Clifford Allen wrote in his *Textbook of Psychosexual Disorders*: 'It seems to me that the essential criterion for normal intercourse is that it is one which tends to fertilize the woman. Intercourse is biologically for this one purpose and any pleasure, excitement, sense of well-being and so on which it produces is merely coincidental and an incitement to do what nature needs to be done' (p. 56). Allen was only saying what needed to be said when what he wrote was still true — that is, when fertilization was 'what nature needs to get done'. The fact is that nature no longer needs either as much fertilization or even the same mode of fertilization. We can deny it for a while, but the youth of the world will discover the potential for planned population through the education that we have given them (Petras, 1973). Once women are recognized as persons fully capable of sexual feeling and not as property, they can no longer be used to satisfy urges as prostitutes, dolls, or wives in bondage. Once women's human right to professional training is provided for in our own schools, as it is now for a few, we can no longer claim that her place alone is in the home. Once the homemaking tasks are shared by men and women, then interpersonal skills will no longer be functionally divided into headwork for men and handwork for women, nor as instrumental activism for men and expressive maintenance for women (Parsons and Bales). Children still need to be socialized, but the task becomes a common one for people sharing a common life-style.

My discipline of sociology teaches me that Catholic doctrine on birth control, abortion and divorce lags behind, even though it follows in the same direction as that of other church groups with less structure and looser decision-making systems — and that all of them are responding slowly to the pressure of population size. The structure of the Catholic Church provides better for the perception of new problems arising from life conditions — such as the conditions of the poor of the world — and accordingly, for directives to respond. It does not provide effectively, however, for the elimination of obsolete forms.

Another thing the theory and practice of sociology reveal is in the area of conditioning. So much that we accept as natural is in fact cultural in origin and as such may be functionally necessary at one time and functionally autonomous at another. No longer necessary for survival, the conditioning usually serves the interest of some group with power to preserve what is to its advantage to retain. This process has been sustained in the past by the timidity with which members call for administrative accountability. Studies indicate that males are more susceptible than females to cultural conditioning, particularly in the area of sexuality. John Petras in an important essay puts it this way: 'It is the rare study in the field of human sexuality that does not report as a fact the greater potential for the sexual conditioning of males as compared to females. Males have been defined as behaving in an environment which has more to offer, symbolically, in the form of erotic stimuli. More recently, we are becoming aware that the prevailing image was due in large part to the assumption that females in Western society lacked a potential for sexual conditioning. It cannot be overemphasized, however, that apart from materials that have emerged from women's liberation, very few individuals have noted this fact. Nearly all the literature has been written by males, and, subtly or otherwise, a definite masculine bias is often reflected' (Petras, p. 59).

Petras predicts for women a potential for greater sexual expressiveness, once they are no longer inhibited by the traditional definition of their passive role in sexual relations, a role reinforced by erotic literature frequently written by men. Knowledge of the more diffuse experience of delight that women experience in their bodies with greater or less intensity has a further implication. It could very well be that the exquisite delight associated with sexual intercourse is a behaviour modification systematically reinforced by taboo and ritual to concentrate human desire on the task of propagating the race as long as that task was functionally necessary for its survival, and that the present de-tabooing and experimentation in the area of sexual behaviour is a preparation for the newer tasks necessary for the preservation of the race. Thus, the universal ideal would no longer be only to live but to develop humanly and to provide that option for all those who choose life. This of course would include the still voiceless poor of the world.

Once a discipline like sociology or anthropology begins to reveal comparatively the changing focus of the sacred, the question arises: what determines the concentration of taboo and ritual in one area as compared with another? In the broadest context, language has much to do with this concentration. Recent research in the area of symbolic interaction teaches us how children are socialized to accept as natural what their parents insist is normal, expected and right (Douglas, 1973; Manis, 1973). Language with special words for status groups teach as normal what is societally structured; in fact, a deference system that is exploitative is preserved by cherished norms. Sociology can demonstrate that 'reality is socially constructed', that 'the processes of social interaction constrict the typifications and recipes which make up social reality', that even the dimensions of time and space are socially constructed, and finally 'that human thought serves human interest'. 'The social configuration of the times are in the thought system' (Douglas, pp. 10-11).

These observations have enormous implications for the new interest of the Church in the development of community, in contrast with the old sacralization of the family. Our theological language is rooted in patriarchal family terms because of the generic masculine. Despite the fact that Scripture admonishes us to call no one father but 'your Father who is in heaven', we have used the word quite freely for heads of families, local churches and countries, and have even permitted business magnates to take a paternal interest in their workers, psychiatrists in their pateints, etc. In every case exploitation has followed. So far has this use of 'father' extended that in some cultures a woman is subject first to her father, then to her husband, and in old age to her son.. This male dominance prevails with no disturbance to the mind-set of the male who allocates the roles. A woman's coming to consciousness of herself as a human being, of the prerogatives that men arrogate to themselves and of their assumptions about women — these processes represent a conscientization that cannot be retracted (Freire, 1970).

Art, literature, professional writings, and religious practice communicate to the public a whole range of rationalizations embodied in cultural materials — including a church liturgy geared to preserve an ascendancy that the Church has now disavowed in theory but not in practice (Daly, 1973; Doely, 1970). For women who have chosen ministry as their life's vocation, the situation presents an enormous task. These women ask: how can a Eucharist which calls forth a transformed community, be celebrated when the image in which it is cast is not community but patriarchal family? They ask further how we can preserve an ecclesiastical structure which is so male-dominated that the thousands of books and reports written by women to show the anomaly of this situation never come under the purview of men. Men still write about and research the priesthood without considering the issue of the ordination of women (Neal, 1974). So concentrated is the question of sexuality on the issues of birth control, abortion and divorce, as well as on the issues of premarital sex and the possibility of a married clergy, that men are not yet aware of the general problem of a male-dominated theological language, liturgy, and the religious education that is denying to women a place to celebrate life in the Church. This problem, already an anguish for a comparatively small number of women, will burst upon our consciousness with a suddenness we will be unable to cope with unless those who dominate the discipline of theology become aware that women are searching the Scriptures in a hermeneutic circle that goes far beyond the issue of unborn life to the issue of human development. Moreover, these women are doing this research with a mandate received directly from their Church (*Gaudium et Spes*; Pope Paul, 1967). Soon they will discover their common oppression with the poor of the world.

Evidence is accumulating that gives the lie to the division of labour into instrumental activism for men and expressive maintenance functions for women. Human personalities are at once both instrumental and expressive, and call for communal structures which provide for development along both dimensions, not as couples, forming a unity when matched together, but as persons, whole in themselves. Aiming for wholeness men and women can do something effective about the contradictions that are present in the proposals that the Church still offers for ethical solutions for problems about life and marriage.

When the right of a foetus to live is affirmed by a body of bishops in clear and unambiguous terms, though the same body could not condemn an unjust war using the same argument, women who bear these foetuses in their bodies and know the history of how they came to be wonder at the arrogant certainty of those who affirm the one while they are too uncertain to condemn the other. In another contradictory position a method of birth control by rhythm has been affirmed from 1936 onward, although even now medical research cannot predict the time of ovulation in the menstrual cycle. Nor do the bishops make research funds available for the continuation of this much-needed research. The 70% of women whose menstrual cycles do not match the bishops' model can only wonder at the intentions of those who propound such 'certainties'. Furthermore, as long as dubious measures are being affirmed, available research on population control is not supported. And finally, the conflict generated between people trained to accept patriarchal dominance will find no adequate resolution in marriage counselling unless the patriarchal model is replaced by an experience of communal participation.

My discipline of sociology in theory and research, and especially my research on the changing structures of religious orders of women, confirms that the major sexual problem for consideration by the Church is the human rights of women in the consciousness of men, men who manage the affairs of the Church without recognition of their sisters whom they need if ministry, theology, and clerical research are to be done adequately. Willingness of women to live in a male-dominated society will decrease rapidly as the rights of *paterfamilias* decline and the implications of full human rights develop. Population size makes it no longer functional to continue subconsciously the social conditioning — operative in art, education, and the mass media — which perpetuates father-rights long after we have rejected them intellectually as inhuman and replaced them at the value level with human rights. When liturgy, church law, and theology celebrate in language and intent this human development affirmed by Council and decree, then men and women can work out together an ethic for control of life. Until then, what theologians do in this area is painful rationalization, reflecting an experience too narrow to have meaning for those not included in the deliberation about the life they bear or intend to bear. Women are demanding control over their own bodies, over their minds, and over their hearts. Men have thought that they themselves had this kind of control but, because of their overrationalized education, what they have falls far short of what is humanly acceptable now that human development which includes the poor of the world has become the intended goal of Church action and reflection.

A Christian perspective on sexuality will be worked out when men and women set their fantasies aside and in communal encounter face the serious questions of life, love, and sacrament. The rules and regulations that will emerge will not resemble the obsolete regulations presently prescribed for men and women with regard to birth control, abortion, divorce and sexual relations outside a context of love. The current system is no longer credible; the time for the creation of the new community is now. The future of the Church rests with those making current decisions in response to the Spirit which is moving all over the land. The problem is rooted in the reality that we are, in gospel terms — a church of the poor — but in historical reality a church that periodically gets captured by those who rule, because they are still the fathers speaking for the children, relatively untouched by the people whose life condition is not yet categorized in sacred language.

Bibliography

C. Allen, *Psychological Disorders* (London, 1969).

Mary Douglas, *Purity and Danger: An Analysis of Concepts of Pollution and Taboo* (New York, 1966).

Mary Douglas, ed., *Rules and Meanings: The Anthropology of Everyday Knowledge* (Maryland, 1973).

Mary Daly, *Beyond God the Father: Toward a Philosophy of Women's Liberation* (Boston, 1973).

Sarah B. Doely, *Women's Liberation and the Church: The New Demand for Freedom in the Life of the Christian Church* (New York, 1970).

P. Freire, *Pedagogy of the Oppressed* (New York, 1970).

Ellen Frankfurt, *Vaginal Politics* (New York, 1973).

'Gaudium et Spes', *The Documents of Vatican II*, ed., Walter M. Abbott, S.J. (New York, 1977), pp. 199-316.

G. Gutierrez, *A Theology of Liberation: History, Politics and Salvation* (New York, 1973).

'Lumen Gentium', *The Documents of Vatican II* (New York, 1966), pp. 14-96.

J. G. Manis and Bernard N. Meltzer, *Symbolic Interactions* (Boston, 1973).

M. E. Marty, *Protestantism*, History of Religion Series (New York, 1974).

J. L. McKenzie, *The Roman Catholic Church: An In-Depth Look at its Structure, Worship, Belief and Works* (New York, 1969), pp. 268-269.

Kate Millet, *Sexual Politics* (New York, 1970).

Marie A. Neal, 'Women in Religion: A Sociological Perspective', *Sociological Inquiry*, 1974 (in press).

T. Parsons and R. Fried Bales, *Family Socialization and Interaction Process* (New York, 1955).

Pope John XXIII, *Pacem in Terris* (NCWC News Service, Washington, D.C., 11 April 1963).

Pope Paul VI, *A Call to Action*: apostolic letter on the eightieth anniversary of *Rerum Novarum* (Washington D.C., 1971).

Pope Paul VI, *Popolorum Progressio*, Encyclical Letter (New York, 1967).

J. W. Petras, *Sexuality in Society* (Boston, 1973).

J. L. Segundo, *Latin American Theology Today: A Theological Method* (unpublished class notes, Harvard Divinity School, Spring, 1974).

Jean Lemaire / Evelyne Lemaire-Arnaud

The Catholic Image of Sexuality as Seen by the Marriage Counsellor

THE professional practice of marriage counselling is of relatively recent vintage, appearing mainly in North America and Western Europe. Its systematic organization is even more recent, as is theoretical reflection on this professional practice. Most often it comes down to intervention of a psychological nature that is sought out by one of the marriage partners. The chief role of the marriage counsellor is to provide psychological help and nondirective guidance. The aim is to enable the client to take cognizance of the image that he or she is conveying to the other partner and to realize the impact of his or her attitude on the partner. In this way the client may be able to step back a bit and alter his or her attitude towards the partner in a salutary way, thereby reducing the initial complaints about the partner that he or she brought to the therapist.

In some instances, and more frequently now than formerly, counselling is sought by the two partners together. This joint consultation enables the therapist to facilitate the flow of communication between the two partners that is often blocked in serious ways. Thus, in addition to the therapeutic benefits for the individual, important aspects of their life together as spouses are freed of obstacles and blocking factors.

There are other forms of intervention as well, but there is no need to dwell on them here. This brief introduction is enough to show the reader that there is a necessary tieup between the professional practice of marriage counselling and clinical psychology. It shows how important it is for the marriage counsellor to be conversant with the principles of psychopathology and psychosociology. It also shows how important and necessary it is for the marriage counsellor to be trained in the perception of the unconscious factors involved in the problems brought up by the client. These unconscious factors are obviously of fundamental importance in the love relationship between the spouses, but they are just as important for the counsellor insofar as he or she wishes to help the client. The marriage counsellor must be able to step back from his or her own desires, prejudices, and guiding norms so that his or her own problems do not get mixed up with those of the consulting client. It should be obvious, then, that the training and formation of the counsellor must include a psychoanalytic orientation, though the counsellor may never practice psychoanalysis as such.

The theory and practice of marriage counselling forces us to take into account the personal norms of the client as well as his or her upbringing, education, philosophical and religious convictions, and so forth. Now insofar as their overall image of sexuality is concerned, Catholics seem to be imbued with a markedly distinctive image that sets them off from other Christian circles in more than one respect. This image is translated into their day-to-day behavior patterns also, particularly when they have been deeply influenced by a traditional Catholic upbringing and education.

What sort of questions is the marriage counsellor prompted to raise about this overall image of sexuality on the basis of clinical experience and professional research? To formulate these questions, one must first recall certain facts that are forced upon one's attention in the course of day-to-day counselling.

Guilt feelings and sexual activity

The most salient fact is that genital activity is freighted with massive doses of guilt. This in itself, it should be noted, is a generalized phenomenon. It is to be found in most cultures, and particularly in the overall complex known as Judeo-Christian culture. But the carryover of this basic fact into behavior is more or less marked among Catholics, and those with a traditional upbringing often allude to the massive presence of such guilt feelings. We also observe that many of them see this guilt diminishing bit by bit after marriage. This means that among Catholics marriage takes on important and distinctive connotations of guilt-removal, so that the psychological significance of marriage is often more important for Catholics than it is for nonbelievers. The psychological and sociological sciences have brought out the importance of different rites and rituals in removing feelings of guilt from various patterns of conduct. One can readily see what this means insofar as Catholics with a traditional upbringing are concerned: more than other people, they have a real need to insist upon this ritual (marriage) and a deep psychological interest in stressing its absolute, irrevocable, and 'sacred' character.

Now this imputation of guilt to sexual activity is a fact which entails both positive and negative consequences for the couple, and those consequences are often interwoven in complicated ways. Among traditionalist Catholics we find that it relates to sexuality as a whole and therefore has consequences on many different levels. Insofar as the short-term preparation for the sexual act and genital activity is concerned, these guilt feelings are noticeably present in the period of foreplay; and we know that foreplay is most important if the sexual act is to signify real communication between the partners. The frequent effect of the presence of guilt feelings during foreplay is to restrict fantasy and imaginative activity, with the result that the partners give and receive less satisfaction during the sex act itself. Many cite this lack of satisfaction in lovemaking with their legitimate spouse as the reason for looking for extramarital sex.

Inhibitory effects of the same sort are produced by the guilt feelings which people sense more or less consciously in connection with acts of tenderness exhibited during the course of day-to-day life. More important, perhaps, is the inhibition surrounding the long-term preparation for genital activity among traditional Catholics, particularly among those of the urban middle class. The progressive discovery of the other person's body and erotic sensibility is often felt to be something sinful, even when the two people have been made aware of the necessity and importance of this fact.

Obviously enough, these inhibitory effects are not found in all. In the last analysis it depends more on the psychological structure of the person involved than on his or her religious affiliation. Certain obsessive tendencies encountered frequently tend to go hand in hand with stress on the guilt-laden nature of sexual activity. These obsessive tendencies would include scrupulosity, mental rigidity, attachment to the letter of the law, and the need for repeated reassurance and verification. They certainly are not the exclusive privilege of Catholics with a traditional upbringing. On the other hand it must be said that they are found more frequently among such Catholics.

These facts seem to have two basic consequences. On the one hand, some people see a connection between their Catholicism and their failure in conjugal or sexual activity. This prompts them to call into question not only the Church's moral teaching on sexual behavior, which was acquired by cultural programming at an early age rather than by personal reflection, but also their religious practice, their adhesion to the Church, and even their faith in Jesus Christ in some cases.

On the other hand, we get a very different reaction. The obsessive traits noted above are experienced, often unconsciously, as defences against anxiety. For this reason many people with those traits are attracted to the more traditional type of Catholicism, whatever their early upbringing may have been. Hence on both fronts there is the likelihood that an ever closer tieup will form between an obsessive psychological structure on the one hand and a traditionalist religious practice on the other.

The choice of a marriage partner

Those observations based on clinical experience cannot help but raise some questions about the overall image or representation of sexuality in the Catholic mind. They tie in with other questions prompted by somewhat more theoretical reflections on the choice of a marriage partner and the process of pairing. To sum up the matter briefly, we might say that the unconscious affinities which underlie, give direction to, and ultimately determine the choice of a marriage partner can be classed in two general categories.

On the one hand the future partner is experienced as satisfying, or as a possible object for the satisfaction of desire. This is the case in any lovemaking relationship, whatever form or legitimacy it may have: e.g., flirting, brief escapade, long-term affair, marital union. On the other hand, however, the choice of a marriage partner has features of its own which distinguish it from other types of love affairs or relationships. They relate to the fact that no human individual is fulfilled or complete, psychologically speaking, and hence each and every human being is spontaneously looking for unity with another. Into this oneness they hope to integrate all their various and divergent tendencies, and thereby protect themselves against those tendencies which they cannot control satisfactorily. It is there where people are weakest that they will tend to expect the other party to reinforce their own defenses. The 'ego' is counting on the 'object' to protect it against the unconscious impulses which it has most difficulty in controlling. Thus the choice of a marriage partner is characterized by marked signs of defensiveness, for the spouse is meant to serve as a barrier against poorly controlled impulses.

Leaving aside pathological cases, then, we can say that the weakest subjects have the greatest need to reinforce their own defense mechanisms. Their defensive needs, then, will induce them to choose a partner and a pattern of conjugal life that will satisfy those needs. Take the case of someone who is weak and fragile, and who therefore is particularly worried about sexual or aggressive impulses going out of control and bursting in upon his or her life. Such a person will be inclined to choose a partner and a lifestyle which strictly limit his or her sexual or aggressive possibilities. People of this sort will latch on to practices that enable them to distance themselves from the body and sexuality. They will likewise tend to latch on to teachings and doctrines which, in their view, extol this distancing. Thus the general image or representation of sexuality in traditional Catholicism is sought out by fragile people of this sort. They marry partners which fit in with their own defensive needs, creating a couple with a very distinctive and even peculiar structure.

Consider, for example, those couples who come for marriage counselling because they have not managed to consummate their marriage. In general they are people who found it very easy to accept the traditional norms, and who did not experience any tension between their own desires and official prohibitions during their engagement period. That, indeed, was the happiest time of their lives; in many instances they prolonged it as long as possible. They are happily and actively involved in all of the educational activities and groups concerned with marriage preparation, but they never give any hint or sign of their inability to consummate their own marriage. By the same token, the 'curing' of the problem often occasions great difficulties for each of them. It sometimes leads to a break with their traditional upbringing and even with each other.

Then there are what might be called the 'idealist' couples, who come for marriage counselling because at least one of them is suffering in some way. The structure of their relationship is also quite distinctive. The defenses of one partner mesh closely with those of the other so that they are completely dependent on one another and completely subservient to the moral law. When their problems are helped, we often find that they break with the norms they had followed in the past.

Women suffering from frigidity will often try to justify their frigidity and reject treatment by appealing to the ill-advised remarks of some member of the clergy who denounced sensual pleasure and the active search for it. It should be pointed out, however, that those who refuse to change their behavior always rely on some moral or logical line of argument to justify their refusal. They will utilize any and all philosophies, cultures, and religions to justify their own position, however neurotic and painful it may be.

All this cannot be a matter of indifference to the Catholic Church. The overall image of sexuality expressed in such behavior patterns is viewed by normal and civilized people as something which established a link between Catholicism and less desirable results: a diminished level of personal growth and fulfillment, frigidity, marital failure and its impact on the offspring, and the imputation of guilt to genital activity and foreplay with all the unfortunate consequences alluded to above.

Contraception and marital life

Suspicion, then, seems to be cast on the value and worth of pleasure as a component of marital lovemaking and as a supporting factor in the communication between the spouses. This suspicion finds expression in attitudes and stances, some of which have been the subject of lively debate. Here we shall limit ourselves to a discussion of a few of them.

One concerns the matter of contraception. For some time fear of excessive procreation has played a real role in limiting sexual relations between husbands and wives. But the contemporary epoch, with its great progress in medicine and biology, has made the problem far more acute, even in areas which are not suffering from a runaway birthrate.

Historians inform us that while there may have been some debate between theologians on this issue, for several centuries the Christianized masses were not very sensitive to, or conscious of, the whole issue of the legitimacy of contraceptives; knowledge of these means were passed on spontaneously by word of mouth. More recently, however, church authorities have taken formal stands on these issues and thus raised questions at the very moment that contraceptives were attaining an effectiveness never before achieved.

Clinicians, then, must be permitted to tell theologians what they have learned from their experience: i.e., the restriction or quasi-prohibition of contraception has played a destructive role in the lives of many couples who have attended to that position. Of course contraception is not officially condemned as such; only certain methods are condemned. In practice, however, it is those methods which are effective and which could provide some real sense of security that are condemned. The so-called 'natural' methods (based on rhythm, infertile periods, and the menstrual cycle) are highly uncertain, but only they are officially authorized. This means that many couples are obliged to give up a large part of their genital activity, particularly in the case of women whose menstrual cycle is not perfectly regular. That comes down to quite a few women, it seems.

We must point up the serious havoc created by this quasi-prohibition. The fact is that it leads to an increase in extramarital experiences and affairs which are surrounded with intense guilt feelings and which seem to have far more serious consequences than similar escapades do in the case of other couples—the latter accepting them with a certain mutual tolerance. The effect on the children is also serious. Even very young children, who are not yet in a position to reason things out, are very sensitive to fluctuations in the communication between husband and wife. They can sense the unvoiced misunderstandings and frictions caused by the prohibition or limitation on physical intercourse between their parents.

Finally, another phenomenon crops up with some frequency in the case of couples who observe the Church's prohibition on effective means of contraception. Finding that they do not really want a child, or that they cannot accept the consequences of bringing a child into this world, they resort to abortions.

Insofar as this whole question of contraception and marital life is concerned, marriage counsellors and therapists who are convinced Christians themselves cannot help but raise certain questions when they see the results produced in Catholic circles by the publication of the encyclical *Humanae vitae*. They can be summed up under three basic heads:

1. Most Christian couples take no real account of the encyclical. It seems to have had no real impact on their marital lives at all.
2. In the case of those who feel that they are concerned about the encyclical, it seems that many of them have made a distinction between what they regard to be the essential part of their faith and what they regard to be a proposed line of moral conduct suggested by the celibate members of the Church. In the case of these people, Rome's document has not had any practical effect on their conjugal lives; but it has diminished the scope of authority which they feel they can accord the Catholic hierarchy.
3. A small number of couples have faithfully and persistently followed the norms laid down by the Pope. In their case the problems cited above have cropped up in significant proportions. And the situation has been aggravated by the fact that clergymen had been very tolerant in this area in the years immediately preceding the papal encyclical.

Premarital sex

Another area in which the general image of sexuality finds concrete expression is the area of premarital sex. In the past, the concern of civil society was the humanization of the child brought into the world; and this concern was backed up by religious authority. It was this concern that justified the traditional family structure and that led to prohibitions against extramarital and premarital conception. Today, however, the generalized use of contraception is reducing the risk of conception more and more; so the Church can no longer justify her prohibition by appealing to a societal necessity which she has transformed into a 'natural' moral law.

Present-day society has evolved greatly and there has been a pervasive change in people's *mores*. This has had an important consequence: it is now much more difficult for people without previous sexual experience to adapt to conjugal and family life. We are not trying to suggest that everything was fine and dandy in an earlier day. We are not saying that there were not major problems of adaptation involved in marrying off ignorant girls to men they hardly knew. But all that did take place in a world where social, moral, and cultural norms remained relatively fixed and stable. Today we find that those who have not had any sexual experience are exposed to greater risks than other people when they become involved in marital life. In our day, for example, virginity is no longer felt to be a great value by most individuals, even in Christian circles. Moreover, societal pressure does not operate to maintain the marriage bond, and sexuality itself is regarded as essential to communication between the spouses. But extramarital escapades and affairs seem to represent a greater danger for the married couple when the spouses have not had any sexual experiences prior to their marriage.

This particular phenomenon is of relatively recent vintage. It also varies greatly from country to country, depending on the pace and scope of sociocultural change in each. Undoubtedly there were other motives behind the moral prohibition against premarital sex than those associated with the more complete fulfillment of the couple and each partner. But we also know that the growth and fulfillment of the children, in whose name marriage is defended, profoundly depends on the quality of the relationship between their parents. It is not divorce as such that causes the child suffering and emotional upset; rather, it is the constant but camouflaged lack of understanding between the parents. Divorce is merely one of the possible outcomes of that lack of understanding. It is often a serious matter, but it is not always the most serious outcome or alternative that might ensue.

Given these circumstances, the marriage counsellor might well question the theologian about the reasons which are offered to justify the prohibition of premarital sex.

Fidelity and extramarital relations

A final area about which questions might be raised by the marriage counsellor is the vast domain of marital fidelity and its sexual expression. The problem is too enormous to discuss in detail here, but we would like to outline it in schematic form.

Statistics from marriage counsellors indicate only a small fraction of their clients come because one of the partners is engaging in extramarital relations; in such cases it is more often the client's partner who is doing this. But we find a large and growing number of cases where such relations are practiced and openly admitted by both. At one point or another, in short, more and more married people are having a sexual relationship with a third party and not concealing that fact from their spouse.

Traditionally the establishment of a sexual relationship with a third party was a matter of the greatest gravity in the life of a married couple, and it often led to a break between them. Today we find that such extramarital relationships are not being experienced in exactly the same way at all. They are important and significant events, to be sure, but what they seem to signify mainly is some difficulty or lack in the life of the married couple. They do not have the overtones of gravity and seriousness which they had in the past, even up to a few short years ago.

In some cases we find that if an extramarital experience is fleeting and of short duration, it has positive effects on the person involved and the spouse once they talk it over among themselves. Obviously this is not the rule. But the point is that if one were asked whether such experiences do irrevocable damage to the couple or rather improve their relationship, one could no longer give a single flat answer to that question. If one wanted to offer some fairly general answer, at the very least one would have to make a clearcut distinction between a passing escapade and a long-term affair.

What seems quite clear is that the important thing is not the sexual side of the experience but the emotional and sentimental aspect. A brief extramarital escapade is not as likely to upset the life of the couple as a long-term relationship of affection and friendship between one spouse and a third party. Thus we might well pose a question to the moral theologian: Is it always proper and correct to stress the sexual aspect when one is talking about the guilt or sinfulness of a relationship with a third party? A certain tradition never attributed guilt to extramarital friendships not shared by one's spouse, though we know from experience that they often brought serious upset to the life of the married couple. Why is there such an exclusive emphasis on the 'sexual' expression or embodiment of the extramarital relationship?

One might also ask whether an extramarital relationship, be it sexual or platonic, is always a sign of a lack of love or attentiveness towards one's spouse. It is not clear that it always is. In some instances an emotional or sexual relationship with a third party can be part of a real process of development. Of course it will call for parallel growth and development in the life of the couple, but the point is that it is not necessarily destructive of their life together.

Finally, experience also shows us the harmful effects of a total lack of opening to the world outside the marriage circle. We find this lack of openness among many couples who are supposedly closely united, and it is often justified by moral arguments. But this lack of openness leads to sclerosis. The two individuals become closed up in themselves and in their narrow circle, contributing little or nothing to the development of their children or their surrounding milieu.

Serious questions facing the Church

This brief recounting of facts should indicate that the general image of sexuality embodied in the lives of Catholics today has negative as well as positive consequences. Because of the negative consequences involved, certain questions deserve to be raised.

Is there not a danger that the Church is transmitting an image of sexuality which was once shared by society as a whole but which is now not? If so, to what extent is that image bound up with anything specifically Christian, and to what extent is it merely bound up with the sociological context of a bygone age? This is a question which must be faced by us all: not only by theologians, marriage counsellors, and psychologists but also by all married couples who must live out their lives in the era of change that now confronts us. Today, more than ever before, there is an obvious split in the lives of Christians between their faith on the one hand and their obedience to the laws of the Catholic Church on the other. It is even more evident with respect to recent laws or norms laid down by the Church.

Marriage counsellors cannot help but wonder when they take note of certain facts. The fact is that a certain pedagogical tradition, inspired by Catholicism and recently stressed by papal decrees, seems to limit some married couples in their self-development and in their ability to live a full married life together. The fact is that some married couples and individuals improve considerably when they give up some of those traditional teachings. The fact is that some are cured when they discover that other people live their sexual lives with far less guilt feelings, and that the latter have not been brought up with Catholic traditions.

A Christian cannot help but wonder when he or she considers certain facts of a similar nature. It seems that some people raised in a strict Catholic atmosphere discover certain fundamental life-values too late— and outside the Church. These values are fundamental insofar as their married life is concerned at least, and their whole life is compromised in some decisive way by the failure to discover those values in time.

If the salt loses its savor, with what will it be salted? Under the inspiration of the Spirit, the theologian has the task of delving into his treasury to discover something that has not yet been made clear or understood. But he must not delay!

To urge him along, we would only mention what we know personally about many marriage counsellors in Europe, and particularly in France. Many of them can look to Christianity and its inspiration as the source of their own vocation. But when they ponder their own professional practice, they cannot help but wonder what has happened to the great gospel message of love. Is it not overlayed with centuries of varied interpretation? Does it not need to be reread and better understood?

Translated by John J. Drury

Klaus Breuning

Responsible Sexuality as an Educational Goal: Problems and Prospects

FOR centuries Christian education has shaped the attitude of the growing child and adolescent to his or her sexuality. This education was characterized by an unbroken living tradition, a sure awareness grounded on faith, and an ethics derived from that faith. For a variety of reasons, people today no longer sense that this traditional value system is universally valid. This feeling is compounded by another realization based on pedagogical reflection. More and more educators are asking themselves whether any educator has the right to have such a determining influence on the shape of the growing child's future life that education becomes little more than the transposition of the educator's own patterns of behavior.

Responsible educators have learned to do more than operate on the basis of their own experiences and value systems. They have learned to take cognizance of their pupils as well, and to realize that the latter may not share their experiences or values. Thus if we want to ponder the goals of sex education and the possibilities of offering help to our students, we must start out from the situation of these young people.

The situation confronting adolescents

We can only delineate the present situation, with all its changed features, in broad outlines here. In fact we must focus on those changes which have some relevance to sex education, relying on the reported experiences of numerous educators in the industrial nations of the Western world. This particular report will concentrate on the data which has appeared in sex-education materials published in the German-speaking world.

The first fact to be noted in this connection is a result of the biological acceleration we find in our culture world: i.e., the growing gap between physiological sex maturity on the one hand and socio-economic maturity on the other.[1] In many industrial areas the age-limit on certain activities has been lowered or is in the process of being lowered now: e.g., the voting age, the drinking age, and the age of legal adulthood. Thus there is some greater recognition of the physiological, intellectual, and psychic maturity of the young person and adolescent as a sexual being. On the other hand, however, there has been no essential reduction in the gap between those factors and the socio-economic potentialities of the adolescent to live his or her sexuality in a personally responsible way.

So far theoretical and practical pedagogy has not come up with very satisfactory answers to this problem.[2] The problem comes to a head when young people openly ask the educator what they are to do with their sexuality *right here and now*. They know the theory well enough. But the problem of their body and their relationship to members of the opposite sex is a compelling one which they experience in very concrete terms every day.

Acceleration is not the only hallmark of the times. Another critical factor is the pervasive 'sexualizing' of the public domain and the media, which has come in for much pastoral criticism. Right off, however, we must recognize that this process is a belated consequence of a deeper underlying tendency that goes back to the Enlightenment and that pervades the modern period of history. Human sexuality, too, is to be stripped of its numinous and purely 'natural' aura. With the help of various scholarly and scientific disciplines, it is to be put at man's disposal. Medicine, biology, psychology, sociology, ethology, and ethnology have expanded our knowledge of human sexuality to almost unimaginable and infinite dimensions. The mass media, informational literature, and pseudoscientific pronouncements have popularized this data in more or less problematic forms. As a result, young people confront an environment in which sexuality is ever present to their eyes and a carefully calculated factor in "the affluent society."[3]

As far back as 1955, Helmut Schelsky pointed out that sexuality had long since become another consumer item.[4] The result is vividly described in a document put out by a Hessian youth group: "Who today sells anything . . . without using pretty legs, luscious lips, and other sex symbols?"[5]

What is the reaction of today's young people to the massive barrage of sexuality to which they are subjected, to the promises of 'love' and 'happiness' that are offered over the sales counter? It seems impossible to make any general or universally valid statements on the matter, but one can mention certain typical reactions that are noticed by today's educator. The general picture we derive from these observations is highly complex and somewhat contradictory. On the one hand many of today's young people display a rebelliousness against their elders which is far more intense than that displayed by earlier generations. This rebelliousness is not confined to the sexual sphere alone, by any means. Today's young people operate on the basis of their own personalized set of norms and behavior patterns, regarding this as proof of their own independence. On the other hand, however, they wittingly or unwittingly are looking for new models and guidelines with which they can identify. On the one hand they protest vigorously against 'church' laws, 'divine' commandments, and 'moral' imperatives; on the other hand they often feel quite unsure of themselves in practicing sexual freedom and open to the whole question of what life as a whole might mean. Many of them strongly feel that their sexual liberation is a mark of self-determination and self-discovery, but at the same time they seem to be equally unconscious of the fact that they have subjected themselves to new restraints. It is also quite apparent and undeniable that some of their forms of sexual activity, carried on in opposition to occupational restraints, school dictates, and the 'performance principle' of the affluent society, are really forms of catharsis. They represent the area of freedom, the breathing space, to which many young people flee in hopes of being themselves. By the same token, however, they often run into constraints and stresses in the latter area that are just as great as the ones from which they were trying to escape.

Complicated and varied as the behavior of young people in this area may be, one thing seems undeniable. From the decade of the sixties on we find an obvious and general liberalizing of attitudes and patterns of conduct with respect to sexuality. This is true even in the case of young people who have come from deeply Christian homes or who themselves are deeply committed to the Church and church practice. Many aspects of this fact have already been confirmed by empirical studies.[6] While people may dispute certain details of these findings,[7] some points now seem beyond question. There seems to be solid evidence that today's young people engage in sexual activities and sexual experiences at an earlier age than did young people before the 1960s; that on the average they engage in these activities more consciously and free of conflict; and that the difference between more highly educated and less highly educated young people in this respect, which once was quite discernible, is no longer relevant at all.

The confrontation with tradition

The above remarks should make it clear that it is basically not a matter of the educator being confronted with a 'new morality' espoused by the younger generation. On the contrary, the aforementioned attitudes and behavior patterns are better understood as an 'anti-moral' reaction. To a large extent the activity of young people is a reaction against the words and actions of priests, parents, and teachers. They are trying to break out of the chains which they feel were forged on them—by their religious education in particular. The reaction can go so far that many young people may not seem to be concerned at all about the role of norms and conscience in this area.

Whether the reaction is justified or not, it cannot be denied that many young people are reacting strongly against everything connected with religion and the Church. Many religion teachers have attested to this reaction in past years. It seems almost impossible to alter the negative image which young people have of the magisterial Church insofar as sexual matters are concerned. This is due to a variety of factors, *Humanae vitae* in particular. The official church has continued to insist on obligatory celibacy for priests and has refused to deal openly with the whole question of what is meant by *viri probati.* On a whole range of critical questions dealing with life today, the Church's hierarchy has taken stands which seem incomprehensible to young people This has convinced them that it is not worthwhile to discuss sexual questions with a 'representative of the Church' in religion classes; for that representative will merely indulge in apologetics for the Church's position.

In the meantime the Church has become the scapegoat for everything that is wrong in this connection. She is criticized mercilessly for burdensome and fateful consequences that really have complicated historical causes. Back in 1963 Alex Comfort could voice this reproach: "The greatest negative contribution of Christianity has been to turn sexuality into a problem."[8] But a later author might well dispute that contention and say: "Christianity bears less of the blame for the typically antisexual attitude of the West than is generally assumed (even by Christian authors)."[9] Societal factors have played an important role in this matter. Consider, for example, the role played by the moral code of a society dominated by the bourgeoisie. Consider the taboos placed on sexuality during the Victorian age, and its emphasis on an antisexual model of uprightness and 'good breeding'.

That is not to deny that the Catholic Church has not left her mark on the attitudes of today's teachers and played a decisive role in arousing the dissent of young people. She offered people a casuistic approach to religion and morality, and she identified her teaching with the bourgeois emphasis on 'respectability'. For decades now, moral theology has sought to update itself and to throw off the burdensome heritage of past tradition.[10] But those who are active in pastoral and educational work cannot doubt the fact that past history still weighs heavily on their shoulders; that it is not yet a thing of the past at all. What passes in many circles as Christian sexual morality is often far removed from what modern biblical exegesis and moral theology have to say about human sexuality. Age-old value systems, attitudes and hierarchies continue to operate on people's minds—bolstered by the force of traditions that are not subjected to ideal reflection.

Here we might cite one example of the continuing impact of traditional moralistic viewpoints and convictions. In certain circles we still find that the sixth commandment of the Decalogue is regarded as the most important one. Moreover, a significant change in meaning and emphasis crept in somewhere along the line. What originally was meant to protect marriage ("Thou shalt not commit adultery") was turned into a much more comprehensive and rather Manichean prohibition against sexual acts in general ("Thou shalt not commit acts of impurity"). While that emphasis has disappeared from more recent catechisms and confessional pamphlets, it has not been corrected in the consciousness (and the unconscious) of many Catholics.

Much the same applies to the narrowing of the whole concept of purity, so that the latter is equated with sexual inactivity and immorality is customarily equated with violations against sexual ethics. Indeed in the education of young children and even in more recent encyclicals[11] we find that an older conception of 'the virtue of purity', which goes back to neoplatonic thought,[12] is still presented as an authentically Christian attitude and outlook.

Against this general background the general uncertainty and insecurity of parents, priests, and teachers is fraught with serious consequences. Many of them find it impossible to master their own past, and a certain kind of religious upbringing must be held responsible for this. If people have interiorized the notion of the 'perduring and immutable teaching of the Church', they will have great difficulty in being open to new insights within that Church. This is all the more true because one's own life-history comes into play when it is a matter of sexuality. Many adults suffered serious pangs of conscience at a critical stage of their growth because they were given to understand that masturbation and certain kinds of touching before marriage were sinful. Such people may not find it easy to be open to a revised moral evaluation of those same phenomena.

The uncertainty of many educators has fatal consequences for practical sex education. It often shows up as an insistent emphasis on moral prohibitions which are not subjected to any reflection. It also explains why many educators appeal to clearcut binding norms as a replacement for personal decision-making. Even more important, however, is the use of anxiety as a tool of sex education. While the public domain offers much enlightenment on sex matters, many educators ultimately resort to fear and anxiety as subtle means of inculcating a sexual ethic. Thus they may warn students against premarital sex by pointing to the serious consequences which might ensue: e.g., conception, venereal disease, and premature cancer.[13]

By now it should be clear that in many respects we need a new approach, one solidly grounded in the Christian ethos, if we are to be able to offer any genuine help. Many people in education and theology have tackled the matter in the past decade. But the fact remains that in no other area is a person so likely to meet with misunderstanding and unfair criticism. Yet in no other area are young people so open to, and anxious for, straight talk and frank discussion. In no area are they more receptive to someone who will make an effort to understand their situation and their difficulties, and who will join them in looking for sound guidelines to orient them in this matter.

Consequences for praxis

A first and important brand of help is solid information on the subject that is suited to the age of the student. Considering the great changes and reactions which the child will experience at puberty, we should make sure that our information anticipates their situation and thus makes it possible for them to develop certain attitudes and patterns of behavior. In contrast to classical sex education, this information should not be restricted to merely biological data; the latter does not adequately cover human sexuality. We must include certain points concerning interpersonal relationships and foster critical discussion and evaluation of alternative ways of thinking, reacting, and behaving.

The goal of such pedagogical help should not be simply that the adolescent comes to know his or her own body. It should also aid the teenager to accept himself or herself as a sexual being and thus find his or her selfhood. This means, of course, that adolescents must also take cognizance of instinctual forces in their lives, realizing that they are subject to certain forms of reaction and response that are not readily controlled. They must learn to take note of their bodily sensations without simply responding to them willy-nilly. Instead they must try to use this awareness as a means of becoming familiar with their self, thereby integrating their sense experiences into their ego consciousness. It is certainly necessary for the adolescent to come to appreciate the possibility and the necessity of saying no to their instincts when reflection and a given situation makes that advisable. That holds true in many areas, not just in sexual matters. But it is also most important that this control and nay-saying be grounded on a basic yes to one's instinctual life. Otherwise one's instincts will never come under control. They will break through into the life of the young person constantly, producing neurotic compulsions and all sorts of unfreedom. The thorny issue of adolescent masturbation points up the necessity of this basic yes to one's instinctual life.

In any case the problem of controlling one's instincts cannot be viewed and solved in isolation. All our pedagogical help should make it clear that it is the task of a lifetime, part and parcel of the larger task of finding one's self. In the last analysis it can only be carried through if a human being overcomes his or her egotistical turning-in upon self by learning to show concrete love for others. We must get beyond the "*homo incurvatus in se*" described by Luther.

To say this, of course, is to propose a broad and comprehensive program of social training and education. It has been seriously neglected for all too long by our 'wrong-headed' pedagogy. Put briefly, the goals of such an education would include recognition of the other as other, acceptance of one's partner as a different person, and a capacity for sympathy and compassion. Thus it would include all those predispositions required to achieve a love relationship. And it need hardly be pointed out that a basically coeducational setup at every level of the education process would seem to be required for such social training. So it seems, at least, from the standpoint of the educational practitioner.

Not to be underestimated in this regard is the importance of making a breakthrough in our conceptual vocabulary. For all too long we have been seriously remiss in working out a clearcut terminology that will not give rise to misunderstandings. As we use words today, denigratory overtones surround the whole area of sexuality. Among adults and parents in particular, sexual realities are obscured under a veil of delicacy which plays down the issues involved. The danger facing theologians specifically is that they will introduce a new sort of mystification by talking about sexuality as if it were something wrapped in mysteriousness and sacredness. Instead theology should present sexuality as that human dimension which has its own particular and special connection with salvation and damnation, with peace and menacing danger, with fulfillment and frustration. Sexuality should be presented as the 'locale' of love, joy, security, happiness, and also forgiveness. The sex organs are organs of contact which make possible the loftiest sort of human communication. They are speech organs through which a human being may share self with another or refuse such sharing, may speak the truth or tell a lie. But such authentic communication does not just happen 'naturally'. It is a life-long learning process and failure is possible all the way along the line.

Now we are not engaging in mystification when we point up the transcendental character of sexuality.[14] With its own peculiar power sexuality directs human beings above and beyond themselves, towards an encounter with a 'Thou'. Not only is this the only angle from which the whole problem of instinctual control can be solved in human terms; it is also the angle which makes clear the supreme goal of any sex education with a Christian orientation. That goal is to introduce human beings to a knowledge and exercise of truly responsible and partner-oriented behavior. Put another way, the goal is to develop in people the ability to give and receive love. It is a long road to travel. Along the route we must make it possible for the young person to overcome the narcissism peculiar to that stage of life[15] and develop his or her capacity for love. We must help them to move step by step towards personal relationships of comradeship, friendship, and intimacy. And at every stage of intimacy we must stress the importance of honesty, personal responsibility, and due consideration vis-à-vis another person.

Today's young people have a keen eye for meaningless conventions and empty facades. Thus they are very well predisposed towards any and all training in honesty and truthfulness. Such training would stress the fact that people must not indulge in pretense with themselves or their partners, thereby raising false hopes or expectations. Training in this concept, then, would be complemented and spelled out more fully by reference to another dimension which is much talked about today: i.e., the dimension of personal responsibility. The latter has come to the fore as a reaction to the older ethics grounded on obedience and subjection to authority. As the teenager grows towards adulthood, he or she must be taught to appreciate and exercise a sense of real personal responsibility in his or her sexual encounters: toward the partner, toward the potential offspring, toward oneself, and toward the society in which one lives.

Sex education of this sort naturally is subject to the incalculable risk involved in the exercise of freedom. If we wish to liberate people for the exercise of mature judgment and personal responsibility, we must be ready to put up with the possibility of mistakes and erring behavior. By the same token, however, training in the responsible exercise of personal freedom does not mean the complete absence of restraints and ties. Indeed only real freedom makes it possible for there to be personal ties and the acceptance of duties and responsibilities.

Today we are becoming more and more aware of the sociocultural underpinnings of norms that have been handed down by tradition. We are also realizing how much they vary from culture to culture. The observance of such norms can provide helpful orientation and relieve people of the burden of making personal decisions all the time. But it cannot be turned into an absolute commandment. Openness and frankness must be encouraged at every level. It is not encouraged when the educator tries to program teenagers in advance by indoctrinating them with traditional norms before they confront some situation calling for a personal decision. This is true whether the programming is negative in the older sense ("Thou shalt *never* do this") or positive in a more recent sense ("Thou shalt *always* do this in the matter of sexuality").[16] The newer approach, stressing some universally valid duty in the realm of sexuality,[17] is just as doctrinaire as the old approach. Both destroy the emancipatory possibilities of sex education. Both are depersonalizing because they reify sexuality into something that can be readily manipulated.

Of course there are insights proper to a given age and stage of development, and corresponding ethical consequences. That does not mean, however, that the educator will work out a highly differentiated moral code based on pedagogical, psychological, and theological data and lie in wait for the teenager. Instead the educator will propose a dynamic morality which does not associate upright behavior with specific concrete acts primarily but rather with the meaningfulness, rationality, and responsible nature of human behavior. The *how* and the *why* are always more important than the *what*.

All norms, laws, and traditions must be judged in terms of their relationship to the law of love, which sums up the Scriptures (Rom. 13:10). The more we adults and our teenagers are set free to shape our lives according to our personal insight and our sense of personal responsibility, so much the more will Christian sexual morality be what it essentially is supposed to be[18]: not a casuistic model of behavior but a summons to personal decision-making. It is in this sense that we can glimpse the whole point in the famous dictum of Augustine: "Love, and do what you will."

It should also be evident by now that sex education cannot be an isolated discipline. It must be an integral part of a total training process in which young people are taught to develop their humanity to the fullest. Sex education is possible only when it is connected with meaningful personal fulfillment in one's life as a whole. It cannot simply be a cluster of isolated insights or the transmission of specific behavior patterns. Our pedagogy and advice will lack force and purpose if it does not lead our students to personal commitment, service to love, and a shift from self-absorption to concern for another.

These remarks should indicate the basic understanding of human sexuality that underlies this paper. Sexuality is both a biological and dynamically instinctual phenomenon on the one hand, and a sociohistorical phenomenon on the other. But it is not a purely natural category on the one hand, nor a purely historical and social product on the other. Any and every attempt to absolutize one of the two poles produces a distorted picture of man. We know that from the testimony of past history and our own day. The real truth is that sexuality is one of those areas in which both elements—predetermined nature and man's shaping of the world in history—clash constantly. There is a permanent tension between them. Precisely because human sexuality lies in the force-field created by those two poles, it poses the opportunity and the duty of self-determination and interpersonal reaction in a critical, ethical way. It is in self-discovery and communication that human life finds meaningful fulfillment.

Translated by John J. Drury

Notes

1. See H. Scarbath, "Geschlechtsreife und Mündigkeit—Liebeserziehung nach der Pubertät," in Haun (editor), *Geschlechtserziehung heute* (Munich, 1971), 32 ff.
2. H. Kentler, for example, proposes the hard and fast thesis that "the here-and-now happiness of the teenager ought not be sacrificed to some future happiness" (in Kentler et al., *Für eine Revision der Sexualpädagogik* [Munich, 4th ed., 1969], 30 f.). His ultimate point is that in the sexual sphere everyone has the right to seek his or her own (egotistical!) happiness and, as circumstances warrant, turn the other person into nothing more than object of sense pleasure.
3. G. Scherer, *Anthropologische Aspekte der Sexwelle* (Essen, 1970), 19.
4. See H. Schelsky, *Soziologie der Sexualität* (Hamburg, 1955), 118 ff.
5. *Hessische Jugend* (put out by the executive board of the Hessischer Jugendring, Wiesbaden), 7/1969, 10.
6. See especially G. Schmidt, "Jugendsexualität und Sexualerziehung," in Haun (editor), *op. cit.*, 53 ff; V. Sigusch and G. Schmidt, "Veränderungen der Jugendsexualität zwischen 1960 und 1970," in Fischer (editor), *Inhaltsprobleme in der Sexualpädagogik* (Heidelberg, 1973), 62 ff.
7. For critical observations on this view, see Scarbath, *op. cit.*, p. 50.
8. A. Comfort, *Der aufgeklärte Eros. Plädoyer für eine menschenfreundliche Sexualmoral* (Munich, 1963), 67.

9. J. van Ussel, *Sexualunterdrückung. Geschichte der Sexualfeindschaft* (Reinbek, 1970), 7.

10. See especially H. Doms, *Vom Sinn und Zweck der Ehe* (Breslau, 1936; French translation, Paris, 1938); withdrawn after Rome stepped into the debate in 1940. See also A. Adam, *Der Primat der Liebe* (Cologne, 1947).

11. Note the use of this concept in the encyclicals *Sacerdotalis coelibatus* and *Humanae vitae.*

12. The notion goes back to Plotinus anyway. It is frequently used in traditional treatises on sexual morality, it being understood as freedom or detachment from "sensual desires." On this point see E. Frhr. von Gagern, *Dynamische Ehemoral gegen altes Gesetz* (Munich, 1969), 41.

13. See G. Siegmund, *Die Natur der menschlichen Sexualität* (Cologne, 1969), 23 ff.

14. See J. Gründel, "Theologie von Geschlechtlichkeit und Liebe," in H. Erharter and H.-J. Schramm (editors), *Humanisierte Sexualität, partnerschaftliche Ehe, erfüllte Ehelosigkeit* (Vienna, 1971), 42 ff.

15. See R. Bleistein, *Sexualerziehung zwischen Tabu und Ideologie* (Würzburg, 1971), 89. In my opinion, he correctly identifies the potential problem of masturbation as one of excessive self-centeredness. Masturbation thus becomes a problem when it is used so excessively that a young person becomes so fixed "on himself, his body, and his own sensual pleasure that his capacity to show love in a relationship with a partner ceases to be functional." If on the other hand we describe an individual act of masturbation as an "incomplete" or "imperfect" act, we can then "encourage young people to explore the reasons why it is imperfect and to get beyond the diminished self-esteem produced by such behavior" (*Ibid.*, 90).

16. See Scarbath, *op. cit.*, 49.

17. S. Haffner in *Deutsches Panorama*, Heft 1/1966.

18. See Bleistein, *op. cit.*, 82.

Josef Duss-von Werdt

The Polyvalent Nature of Sexuality*

IN the overall context of this volume my stated theme represents a crucial highpoint. It is meant to counter the monovalent conception of sexuality which dominates and pervades the official teaching of the Catholic Church and her magisterium. This official church teaching establishes an equation between 'sexuality' and 'procreation', and then links the two together in matrimony. Conciliar texts in a different vein are not integrated into this ecclesial teaching.

Critical study based on the inductive natural and human sciences does not support any such equation. Their findings indicate that sexuality extends far above and beyond procreation alone. The aim of this article, however, is not to ascertain what exactly is the truth with regard to the basic issue raised. Its aim is more on the phenomenological level, seeking to provide *a systematic description of the multi-dimensional import and meaning of sexuality* insofar as that can be ascertained from human experience and scientific study.

I. ANTHROPOLOGICAL PREMISES

Even a descriptive approach to this matter is grounded on one or more anthropological presuppositions about sexuality which enter into our interpretation and evaluation. Such presuppositions, of course, must be constantly checked against empirical findings. Consider the bipartite and

*This article is dedicated to Stephen H. Pfürtner.

tripartite conception of man, for example. The former divides man into body and soul; the latter divides man into body, soul, and spirit; both relegate sexuality to the realm of the body. In their framework, then, all manifestations of sexuality must be relegated to the lowest rung on the hierarchical ladder which they have set up. There is really no room for any sexual psychology or any sexual pathology. Moreover, insofar as human beings are regarded as a montage of components in which the parts exist *prior* to any integral Whole, and of which the sexual elements derive from subhuman nature, sexuality is exiled completely from the 'authentically human' sphere.

But suppose we view *homo* as a Whole or Totality, as an indivisible unity which is not just a juxtaposition of parts. In that case sexuality is an integral part of this totality just as motion and speech are; like the latter, sexuality also has something to do with man's soul and spirit. No longer situated in some readily discernible substrate, it pervades the whole human being from top to bottom; man's psychic and bodily features become different aspects of an indivisible Whole.

That is the basic anthropological premise which will serve as the basis for my following remarks, and which will also be elaborated along the following lines: *From birth on homo is a sexual being, a male or female human being. Homo* does not *have* sex. *Homo is* a sexual being. Thus humans do not start out as some neuter being to which a sexual 'disposition' is appended. All the actions of a human being are the actions of a sexual being, even when they are not of a sexual nature themselves. We do well, then, to make a distinction between 'sex' (German *Geschlecht*; French *sexe*) and 'sexuality' (German *Sexualität*; French *sexualité*), the former referring to man's overall sexual nature, the latter to the sphere of sexual behavior in the strict sense. The fact that *homo* is a being with sex is the underlying basis for the way in which he lives his life in and through sexual behavior.

II. SEXUALITY: A CROSS-SECTIONAL VIEW

On the basis of the above premises I shall now attempt to spell out various semantic dimensions of sexuality without evaluating them.

Three general aspects or directions

Insofar as behavior and concrete experience are concerned, sexuality can be described in terms of three general aspects or directions.

(A) It is *an intrapersonal experience* with a specific content. It entails sexual desires, fantasies, dreams, sensations, stimuli, pleasurable feelings, feelings of anxiety, and reactions of joy or disgust. They may arise spontaneously, or they may be evoked by real or imagined persons and objects. Their meaning and import for the individual depends on many facts: his life-history, his here and now situation, and his inner and outer experience.

(B) It is *a pattern of behavior towards oneself* with a definite and specific content. The individual may accept or reject his bodily reality and sexuality. He may engage in autosexuality without a real-life partner, stimulating himself through imagination or active masturbation, and so forth.

(C) It is a pattern of behavior with its own specific content *vis-à-vis other persons and/or objects.*

Even the sexually continent human being lives and acts in the above terms. Only a human being without sex could be asexual, and such a being does not exist.

Four functions of sexuality

Cutting across the aspects described above, we can identify another cross-section which has to do with the functions of sexuality. Here the above dimensions find partial realization at least and also can be given some valuation. I shall simply list the following as important.

(a) *Sensual pleasure* through contact, stimulation of the senses of sight and hearing, love play, orgasm, etc.
(b) *Release from tension* and satisfaction as the result of genital or extragenital experience of a pleasurable nature.
(c) *Relationship* in a general, relatively nonspecific sense. This might range from affection and love to outright aggression. This 'social' function of sexuality has countless varieties and stages of intensity, including ecstatic fusion on the one hand and complete rejection of sexuality and love on the other. It takes in all the various forms of human association and dissociation: e.g., war, conflict, misanthropy, misogyny, discrimination against sexual minorities, and so forth.
(d) *Procreation.* There are temporal limitations on its realization, not only in terms of the life-history of the individual but also within the age-period when procreation is possible. By contrast, the first three functions mentioned just above are life-long ones. Thus sexuality means more than procreation even in the generative stage of life. Indeed procreation is not any form of sexual experience at all; rather, it is merely a possible consequence of such experience when and if certain biological preconditions are met. It is wholly

independent of any interhuman quality or feature, and also of any individual experience. All children are not the 'fruit' of love—not by a long shot. Even if one wants to produce a child, that intention alone will not do the trick. Thus procreation lies on a completely different plane than do the three aforementioned functions of sexuality.

My listing has nothing to do with a hierarchical ordering, although a mere glance suggests clearly that the hierarchy rooted in Catholic tradition—but not solely in that—has been turned upside down. We usually find sense-pleasure ranked last, if it is included at all. If stress is placed on the primacy of procreation, that is logical enough insofar as one considers the complete unimportance of female orgasm in the procreative act. Procreation requires male orgasm, and that is all. Here we see a very discriminatory view of the female surfacing. She is condemned to a passive sexuality. Ethnologically speaking, we find that the sexual act is described in martial terms. The enemy is taken; the inferior being submits to the superior being. Passive sexuality on the one side is linked up with aggressive, sadistic sexuality on the other side. The two go together.

Now the aforementioned functions are bound up with a human person. This does not mean that they are and can be realized only in a person-to-person encounter. Here I simply mean that they are autosexual, homosexual, or heterosexual. This would include various relationships to things and objects (e.g., fetishism) in which the object represents some desired person. But sexuality can also be stripped of the personal element and reified. As such it is becoming more and more a factor in economic life and business activity. We find it in advertising, movies, and the print media; and it can show up in an almost endless variety of forms. 'Hardcore' pornography, for example, concentrates directly on the genital sphere itself, on first-level sexuality. Advertising and salesmanship tend to concentrate on second-level sexuality (nudity, the secondary sex characteristics, etc.); but they also transpose sexual qualities to such things as cars and cigarettes. The latter might be called 'third-level' sexuality.

Obviously enough, the things which I have just lumped under the notion of reified sexuality cover a wide area and represent a complex amalgam of very different valences. The consumption of pornography, for example, might be regarded as a vicarious substitute for a sexual relationship that is not possible. (It is quite likely that crusades against 'smut' are much the same thing.) In advertising and promotion, woman is reduced to a female sex object. And movies continue to reap profits from the unspoken implications of moral dualism: "Bodily lovemaking borders on the forbidden and is sinful, and is therefore so enticing and attractive!"

Some conclusions

If we take a brief look back over this section and consider it in terms of our basic theme, we can conclude that sexuality has many different valences and meanings; and that none of them is independent of what the human person makes of sexuality. In other words, *it all depends on what sense and meaning a person gives to his or her own sexuality.* Human sexuality does not have any meaning *in itself.* Even its generative aspect is endowed with meaning by the human being. If procreation is my intention, that intention does not lie in 'Nature'. It comes from me, who may want to 'carry on' the human race, the tribe, or the family name. Others may want a child to 'save their marriage' or to give bodily expression to their love.

If procreation is not intended but results nevertheless, then sexuality can have any one of a thousand meanings. None of those meanings derives from nature; they derive from human beings and their many-layered structure. Even when we try to tap the natural sense or meaning of sexuality, we are forced to realize that it is *homo* who determines that meaning. Nature tells us nothing as to what *she* is; it is man who says what she is. Nature is mute! Does that not make it clear to us how wholly responsible we are for our sexuality?

III. THE CHANGING MEANING OF SEXUALITY IN THE LIFE OF THE INDIVIDUAL

If sexuality is linked up solely with procreation, then obviously we can only talk about the 'sexuality' of those who have reached puberty. Sexual maturity, then, must be strictly confined to the *potentia generandi.* Viewed in such terms, female sexuality exists between the approximate ages of thirteen and forty-eight whereas male sexuality exists from about the age of sixteen to death.

Sigmund Freud was not the first to 'discover' the sexuality of children and spread the news to the world. It had been around forever, but people simply had not taken any special notice of it. What Freud did really was to point up the blocks erected against this perception. Whether one agrees with his theories or not, it seems that we must accept one basic supposition as a result of our anthropological starting point. We must assume that sexuality pervades the whole life of the individual from birth to death, finding fulfillment in various ways as man, a sexual being, moves through the various stages of life.

If that be true, then sexuality cannot signify or mean exactly the same thing in each and every phase of life. That is true both objectively and subjectively. It cannot mean the same thing whether we are talking about the normal course of human development or about the structured life-history of a given individual with certain genetic endowments.

In basic developmental terms we can distinguish between a pregenital and a genital phase. The former runs up to puberty, at which point the second phase begins. This division itself is too broad, however, because each phase contains numerous subdivisions. Thus the sexual functions of sensual pleasure and relationship play a great role in the life of the small child, whereas its sexual experience is very diffuse and nonspecific when compared with the genital sexuality of the adult. It is not localized in the sex organs as it is with the adult. (Freud's division into oral, anal, and genital phases is misleading. The terms, insofar as they designate specific organs, cannot be taken at face value.) On the other hand, it will not do to turn the child into an 'asexual angel' who is innocent of guilt in this area; for then we are turning the child into a being without sex, into a neuter creature. It is also inadmissible because we are then measuring the child solely in terms of procreative sexuality as practiced by adults. Underlying this view is the general tendency to set childhood innocence over against adult culpability, and to associate the latter with sexuality. That may be the real reason why people are unwilling to notice sexuality in the life of the child.

It is not my purpose here to describe the course of sexual development in the life of the individual. The point is that the various dimensions and functions of sexuality, which were briefly outlined above, are not equally present and functional in every stage of life. Sexuality is ever present, to be sure, but its objective and subjective import undergoes changes in each stage of life. Hence we cannot define sexuality 'in and of itself', dissociated completely from the life-stage or age of the human person. In each stage of life sexuality has its own intrinsic possibilities and lines of meaning.

Some examples may be of help here. The small child is objectively incapable of procreation. But if it is to be sexually mature later on, if it is to be capable of a sexual relationship and intercourse, it needs to experience the pleasure of skin contact and physical forms of attention and tenderness. The sexual interest and concern of the adolescent is focused primarily on the discovery of self: "Who am I as a man or a woman?" This discovery of one's self and one's sexual identity is a necessary precondition for experiencing another human being as 'other' in a later sexual partnership. Later on in the life of a woman, when she reaches menopause and can no longer bear a child, this may have a profound impact on her feelings of self-worth and self-esteem. Sexuality poses new problems for her when she clearly realizes that she cannot have any more children. Clinical findings indicate that menopause may also create serious problems for the male and his partner-bound sexuality. He may come to feel that his wife is no longer of any sexual use.

The complex nature and meaning of sexuality in the course of human life can be viewed from two different standpoints. One focuses on the individual: e.g., various theories of psychosexual development. The other standpoint focuses on the sociocultural aspects of sexual development: e.g., the work of Erikson and Plos on adolescent development. This latter standpoint has become an object of study much more recently. For a long time the sociosexual side of growth and learning was seriously neglected. Only conspicuous phases of that process were considered at all: e.g., pair formation leading to marriage and the growth of the pair bond in marriage. The steps which led up to that were not given much consideration by psychology; and what those steps should be ideally were hardly noted at all by pedagogy. This probably had something to do with the fact that sexuality was associated wholly with the adult in the 'prime of life'. Old people and children were considered to be asexual.

IV. THE SOCIOCULTURAL FRAME OF REFERENCE

Here we might note in passing that the observations made so far were designed to break up the narrow equation of sexuality with procreation. Now that is very much a problem peculiar to the Western world. The polyvalent nature of sexuality takes on many tints and hues when we look at the traditions of other culture worlds. In one culture the connection between sexuality and procreation may go completely unnoticed; in another culture the elements of play and sensual pleasure may occupy the foreground. In such instances we are obviously dealing with very different anthropological presuppositions. Indeed we can find much of this in our own tradition, though we may have to dig a bit to get to it. In Greek culture, for example, we find the Dionysian emphasis on sensual pleasure existing alongside a rationalistic denigration of the body.

Every culture has its own sexual norms—another indication that there is no natural self-regulation of sexuality. These norms apply to the same realities only in the most formal terms: e.g., to marriage, incest, and homosexuality. In content, however, they differ radically from one another. So we find very different forms of marriage, very different evaluations of premarital sex, and very different evaluations of incest. In so-called 'primitive' cultures we still find a close connection between religion and sexuality as well as between concrete experiences of both types. In our Western culture that tieup still exists only insofar as sexuality is linked up with moral behavior, the relationship being a negative one for the most part.

In general, norms have the function of giving order to society and politics. They can also be used as a means of wielding power. It is quite surprising to note that all totalitarian and authoritarian regimes advocate a strict sexual morality, in which sexuality somehow or other is subordinated to some 'higher' goal. The monovalent conception of sexuality held by the Catholic Church should also be examined and checked out from that standpoint.

V. SEXUALITY AND MARRIAGE

These anthropological considerations of sexuality, combined with a brief overview of the life-history of the human individual, have led us to conclude that *homo* is not just a being with sex but a thoroughly sexual being. *Homo* cannot behave in a nonsexual way. Each and every human being lives his or her sexuality in some way or another, whatever their legal status may be in the matter.

Getting more specific, we can say that we are normally talking about the sexual encounter between adult men and women. Now there are good grounds for maintaining that this encounter is best taken up in an enduring relationship between the two sexes. Even Wilhelm Reich, who was a vehement critic of marriage *qua* institution, saw in *de facto* marriage the ideal possibility for a fully satisfying heterosexual life. Thus the decisive factor in a successful sexual relationship is not marriage as such, but a specific quality of the relationship between the sexes; and this quality is not dependent on marriage.

The linkup between sexuality and marriage in civil law and canon law attests to a prevailing concern for the generative aspect of sexuality. Sexuality is not provided with institutional security for its own sake. Marriage is institutionalized for the sake of the children that might result from a sexual relationship between a man and a woman. In other words, marriage is designed to exercise control over procreation rather than over sexuality as such.

The basic result is that all of marital sexuality and its corresponding morality are subsumed under the primacy of procreation. The monovalent nature of sexuality is set up as a universal principle dominating marital morality as a whole. That is what happened in this century when the Church spelled out her doctrine concerning the ends of marriage. And this tacit assumption is widely held beyond the borders of the Church as well.

Insofar as the Church's position is concerned, Vatican II made some faltering steps in the direction of a more polyvalent conception of sexuality within marriage (see *Gaudium et spes*, n. 50 ff.). It discussed sexuality as an expression of love, and associated that function with the function of procreation. But it did not go so far as to attribute a value of its own to that particular aspect of love.

The integration of a polyvalent conception of sexuality into marriage is required for more than one reason. The procreative period of a marriage is limited in time, and the procreative capacity itself must be controlled and guided. We must also take due note of solid anthropological grounds for a polyvalent conception of sexuality and realize that the duration of marriages today varies greatly by comparison with those of an earlier time. One need only allude to the implications of sexuality for the psychic and marital health of older people to realize that one is broaching a tabooed topic.

It would be a complete distortion of history to maintain that earlier generations failed to take account of the multidimensional import of sexuality and subordinated all their sexual activity to procreation. The existence of a 'double standard' for males is enough to dispel any such idea. It implied, among other things, that the various connotations of sexuality were divided up among different women. One's married spouse was seen in 'monovalent' terms as the mother of one's children; other women would serve as love partners, sexual playmates, and *innamorate*. If we now try to incorporate these many and varied connotations into marital life, then the semantics of marital sexuality will have to be broadened considerably.

Another important matter comes up here in connection with marriage and sexuality, I pointed out above that we must consider people's sociosexual development as well as their psychosexual development. Step by step the two sexes gradually learn to approach each other more closely as they develop. This *rapprochement* also includes their sexuality as such, and it is practiced in sexual partnership. Objections to such a rapprochement and its exercise usually stem from the fact that the whole matter of sexuality among young people is restricted to the issue of premarital sex. Empirical data certainly testifies to the frequency of premarital sex; but it also tells us something about the quality of such relationships. The predominant feature is a pair-bond very similar to that found in a traditional monogamous relationship. Such relationships tend to be characterized by exclusivity and fidelity. If we view sexuality as something that has meaning throughout the life of the individual and that cannot be restricted to the possibility of coitus, then we must fashion models of sexuality for children and adolescents; and our pedagogical models cannot be based solely on the principle of postponement. Such models must do justice to the facts and realities that mark each specific stage of human development. If they do, we might forestall many sexual problems that tend to crop up later in marriage.

VI. HOMOTROPY AND HETEROTROPY

This cursory description of sexuality would be incomplete if it did not take in the matter of homotropy. Here the term refers to that sort of homosexual inclination of which the causes are as yet unknown to us, but which is present as a real, constitutional orientation to people of the same sex as truly as is the orientation towards people of the opposite sex. The point which must be stressed here is that we must view this matter in a far more differentiated way than we have in the past. Flat statements and wholesale condemnations are out of order completely. At the very least we must distinguish between the following sorts of homosexuality: the homosexuality of growing children and adolescents as a developmental phase; the homosexuality resulting from inhibitions with regard to people of the opposite sex; the inauthentic homosexuality of people who are really heterosexuals but who engage in homosexual prostitution; the homosexuality conditioned by circumstance (e.g., by prison life); and the various forms of homosexuality which cannot be measured against heterosexual patterns and which therefore can be regarded as defective or deviant. As I just noted, we know very little about all this. We should not underline this ignorance with moralistic judgments and dogmatic pronouncements.

VII. POLYVALENCE AND CHRISTIANITY

If we go back to the authentic wellsprings of Christianity, we will find no real basis or support for a monovalent conception of sexuality. In fact those sources do not offer us any conception of sexuality at all. What they do offer us is a hint as to what a whole human being is and might be. *Homo* is a created reality who takes hold of his or her sexuality and, as a unified totality, invests the whole import of personhood in a vertical relationship with God and a horizontal relationship with other human beings. It is from that center that we must grasp and appreciate the valences of his or her sexuality.

To put it another way: the sexuality of a given person acquires its sense and meaningfulness from that person. The implied note of responsibility does not stand over against some other category on the prehuman or subhuman level. Rather we are dealing with a radically personal category here. The norm of sexuality is the created human being standing before God and his fellows.

Translated by John J. Drury

Jacques-Marie Pohier

Pleasure and Christianity

IF sex were only a function of biological reproduction, it would not pose such major moral problems. It is sexual pleasure, in fact, which is problematic, and, indeed, pleasure itself (though one might say that all pleasure is in a way sexual). There are a few Christian authorities who teach, like Aquinas, that the pleasure obtained through sexual activity would have been even greater in a world not rendered imperfect by sin, but there are many who teach that the Christian ideal would be to eliminate all sexual pleasure from sexual activity, or even to eliminate all sex.[1] For centuries, Christians have considered pleasure and sex as facts posing major problems; that Christianity should be especially wary in regard to them; and that it had the means to resolve them.

Today there are not a few believers who, like a large number of unbelievers, think that the attitude of Christianity to pleasure and sex is no less problematic than pleasure and sex themselves. If that is so, the greatest contribution that Christianity could make to the solution of the various problems that pleasure and sex seem always to have set, would be to resolve the problem posed by the attitude of Christianity to pleasure and sex. Does this attitude respect the human truth of pleasure and sex? Or the truth of the Gospel as the Holy Spirit announces it to believers today?

To answer these questions, we could retrace twenty centuries of Christian history in order to study the various influences which have played a part in the evolution of Christian talk about pleasure and sex.[2] We could also compare the attitude of Christianity to these matters and its possible antinomies and contradictions, in view of what various disciplines (philosophical, psychological and sociological) teach us about the antinomies or contradictions at the root of the processes by means of which the human being realizes himself (and is realized) as the subject of desire, pleasure and sex.[3]

I. SEX EDUCATION

In 1973 the French government made sex education compulsory in secondary schools. Courses had to be arranged for teachers of the new classes. They were also necessary for priests and religious as well as laypeople teaching in private schools approved by the State. The organizers of one of these courses asked me recently to give a theological lecture on the Catholic faith and sex education.

My argument was roughly as follows: You are all experienced teachers and keen on teaching. You all know for example that to be a good mathematics teacher there are two essential conditions which are independent of your degree of competence in mathematics: (1) you have to like mathematics and take pleasure in doing math; (2) you have to want the people who are to be taught to like math too and to take pleasure in doing it. These two conditions are necessary for all education in any discipline or subject or activity. The same therefore should be true of sex education. The two preconditions for all sex education are: (1) to like sex and to find pleasure in it oneself; (2) to want those one is going to teach to like sex and to take pleasure in it.

However, I said to my audience, many people seem to refuse to apply to sex education these two conditions which they would agree are prerequisites of all other education. Is that legitimate? Can it be derived from what Christianity teaches us about human beings, pleasure and sex? Has Christianity specific reasons for being against Christian teachers starting sex education from these two preconditions, which are quite valid from a Christian viewpoint, for any other form of education? I tried to show that Christians were not so faithful as might be thought to their belief in a God who has created and saved mankind if they thought it was all right to use that faith to say that those conditions did not apply to sex education. I said that Christian teachers who wanted to carry out a healthy sex education should ask themselves what in Christianity made them so sure that, as soon as sex came into question, it wasn't advisable to love the reality to which people were to be educated and to take pleasure in, nor to want those being taught to love it and to take pleasure in it.

Among the many lectures that I have given to very different audiences and sometimes on very controversial subjects, this particular one was undoubtedly that which encountered the greatest resistance from a large part of the audience, and which brought me an immense correspondence which included more indignant or critical letters than I usually receive.

II. THEOLOGICAL INQUIRY INTO PLEASURE

One of the theological reviews which devote each issue to a particular theme recently did a number on pleasure. *Lumière et Vie* is a French journal which is far from timidly conservative. Sometimes it takes the spirit of research beyond what some people think are the outer limits of orthodoxy. For instance it published an issue on abortion, containing an article which did not wholly agree (that is the least one can say) with the position of the Catholic hierarchy.[4] It is a journal which takes every care to criticize the faith on the basis of its own demands.

A good example of this is to be found in the two issues comprising the number on pleasure. That for summer 1973 on knowing and believing, in which the editorial informs us that the theological and ecclesial renewal arising from the last Council is more of a piece of window dressing of the establishment than of a new way of living and thinking; and the issue for November-December 1973 on prophetism, where, after several exegetical articles on the prophetism of yesteryear there is a series of articles attacking in a very practical manner the practices and pronouncements of various national churches, with in general a very harsh diagnosis of the prophetic quality of those Churches offered by some of their memebers. Even though I have tended to approve and sometimes to contribute to these manifestations, I cite them not by way of approval but in order to show that an issue on the subject of pleasure forces a journal to adopt something different to its customary tone.

First of all there is an article in which a psychoanalyst presents the findings of Freudian metapsychology on pleasure. It isn't a neutral article by any means, but that accords with traditional psychoanalytical thinking. Then there is a study of the community as the locus of pleasure, which is concerned with practical research into community life, lay and religious. The articles focuses on a very severe criticism of the pleasure-seeking which is said to characterize such enterprises, one which is wholly oriented to the utopia of a prelapsarian paradise. This communitarian dream shows its true nature in various instances of very primitive forms of authority and power, by a very pregenital form of sexuality, and in an inability to integrate time and change and to adapt to mutability: an inability resulting from excessive orientation to the immediate moment and from discontinuity. Then there is an article on contemporary ideologies of pleasure. Under the heading of 'Freudo-Marxist Activism', Reich, Marcuse and Deleuze are cited as liberation idealists. The author broadens his attack to present all contemporary ideologies of pleasure as despicable by-products of neocapitalism, with an aside on the way in which the underground movement has been taken in and tarred with the same brush. We are told that all this arises from the masochist orgy or the arrogant melancholy of the 'psy' movement. Behind the call for pleasure there is an evil illusion of happiness — a view of happiness hardly shared by theologians like Aquinas who defined man's moral life as a search for happiness (for them the end of man), but certainly shared by, for instance, Dostoevsky.

Then there is a study of Christianity as inimical to pleasure, in which several modern thinkers are cited. We are told that the present state of historical scholarship does not allow us to draw up the balance sheet in regard to the contribution made by Christianity to happiness and to contempt of the world, nor to answer a question about Christian masochism. We are offered some of the schemata which the Church has often used to conceive the reality of pleasure, but we are warned that they vary considerably in their relevance to the essential Christian message: avoidance of temptation, Christian angelism, contempt for the body, dolorism, and so on. Yet the section ends with a reference to something which cannot be considered as part of a 'Christian allergy to pleasure': namely, the mystical tension inherent in the Gospel which invites us to repress desire in limited things in order to affirm its infinity.

The issue in question ends with an article by a religious who is also a psychoanalyst on 'pleasure and joy', with a final section on psychoanalysis, the Church and pleasure. Even though, as he says, neurosis and fear of life can find in religion a rationalizing system which denies pleasure and death, and even if it is true that the Church has often tacitly connived at that view of things, the Church and psychoanalysis do affirm something very important: that is, that pleasure leads to death. The Church says so firmly, for 'the experience of mortification in action to which man is subject throughout his life is the cornerstone of Christianity'. I think that the author is following Jacques Lacan here. Yet most readers of *Lumière et Vie* will understand something quite different here, for they are more used to the connection that Christian morals and spirituality make between pleasure and death, than to Lacan's view of them. But even if that is not so, it is still quite true that this is the first time that a whole issue of *Lumière et Vie* has presented this particular emphasis. When considering a subject that the Church is often accused of rejecting and condemning, and that is thought to be very important by several contemporary thinkers, the first reaction of *Lumière et Vie* is not usually to attack those criticisms or accusations but to consider them responsibly for the benefit of Christianity. But in this case exactly the opposite happened, for the first time in the history of the journal. When I quizzed them on the subject, the editors told me that this was neither voluntary nor conscious.

III. THE PLEASURE OF BELIEF

Good Friday, 1974. In my priory, during the celebration of Jesus' death, which follows the traditional liturgy of the adoration of the Cross and of Jesus, we included a series of dialogues in small groups. Several members of one of these groups expressed their joy at the fact that God was as he was and that he loved men as the event we were celebrating showed he did. One elderly woman said: 'I'm so pleased to be a Catholic that I should like to give that pleasure to others.' A few minutes later, another woman said approvingly: 'What you said just now is very unusual. Especially on Good Friday, it's strange to talk about pleasure, even the pleasure of belief.' At that point, a young man who hadn't said a word up to then, stated emphatically: 'In the Catholic faith there's no question of pleasure; it's all renunciation and sacrifice. Especially on Good Friday.' Then the group turned to another topic.

IV. ORIGINALITY OF THE GOSPEL

Once you begin to think about it, you're struck by the number of facts which are more or less analogous to those I have just mentioned. Often, even during a lecture not directly concerned with sex or pleasure, I have noted that the word 'pleasure' is enough immediately to elicit requests for an explanation. In regard to the religious life, I have said that the vocations crisis would be quite a different affair if there were more religious who obviously lived their religious life as if they did it for the sake of the pleasure it gave them. There have always been people who have asked what pleasure meant. Clearly the word meant something to them in everyday life. Everyone knows what he means when he says: 'That's unpleasant', or 'I don't like that', or 'That's a real pleasure'.

However, when I used words whose meaning wasn't so obvious and direct (such as eschatology, redemption, grace, Trinity), questions were hardly ever asked about them (even though, they often directly concerned the basic topics of my lectures). But questions were almost always asked about the word pleasure, which seems to connote something very mysterious and to pose so many problems in practice.

If there is one thing that psychoanalysis has succeeded in showing, it is that pleasure arouses extreme conflict in a human being. That is why I do not claim that Christianity alone is having difficulties in regard to pleasure. Some modern ideologies are extremely naive to think that pleasure could be experienced without conflicts for individuals and societies. This seems inherent in the human make-up if we think of man as necessarily expressing his desire within a framework of frustration and joy. But however universal the problem posed by pleasure, it takes a particular form in Christianity.

Even though psychoanalysis has shown the radically conflict-ridden nature of the human relation to pleasure, it has also shown us that pleasure is a special object of repression, and how that repression has occurred in a dissimulation of the actual though latent content of an action or pronouncement: that is, beneath its apparent content. But Christianity has probably never been aware of the exceptional nature of the problem posed by its attitude to pleasure. Christianity, in fact, has good reasons for not wanting to be aware of everything the world might say about it, and for wanting to hide beneath refined rationalizations, and even Scripture.[5]

Perhaps a comparison will help here. Imagine someone doing something that everyone else thinks is really odd. Perhaps he washes his hands fifty times a day. Everyone sees quite clearly that something odd is happening, but everyone is also aware that the person in question has some system of explanation and justification for his conduct, and appeals in a quite logical way to ideas or facts: the high degree of pollution, the risk of catching an illness . . . In such a situation, we know there is no point in discussing the alleged reasons for the hand-washing. The real problem is latent and already half-resolved when it comes to the surface: that is, when the individual in question discovers that he has a problem, and that the actual though latent substance of the problem was not what he worried about as the actual problem (the fact of pollution or infection).

After spending several years on the problem of pleasure and Christianity, I would say this. Christianity has a unique problem in regard to pleasure. Everyone round about sees that there is a serious problem. But everyone also sees that Christianity has a system of explanations and justifications for its theories and practices in regard to pleasure. It is a system which appeals logically to the unique affirmations of the Gospel on all areas of human life: on pleasure and sex; the originality of the eschatological interpretation of the conditions of human existence; the originality of Jesus Christ about the meaning of the difficulties of human life; the originality of the Cross, and of Christian renunciation; and so on. All the events and facts to which I have referred are essential Christian realities. The discovery of infection through microbes and pollution seemed very strange (think of Pasteur) and awakened a great deal of resistance. But when the man who washes his hands fifty times a day justifies his odd conduct by citing the actual problems of pollution and contagion, he is alone in confusing two categories of problem; he is the only one to confound the two categories, and to want to hide the oddness and seriousness of his conduct under the veil of the originality and seriousness of such problems.

The problem is half-solved when the discovery is made that the problem isn't actually where people locate it. Christianity's problem in regard to pleasure will be half-solved when Christians recognize that their attitude to pleasure poses a problem whose real content is repressed and denied by trying to hide it under the uniqueness of the Gospel.

If the least experience shows that there is little point in discussing things on the level of the 'problems' asserted by a process of rationalization and resistance, that least shows too that there is little point in explaining to the patient what the latent but real content of his outward talk and behaviour is, or how his rationalization and negation work. In many cases, all one does is to reinforce defences and repression. But experience also shows that when the mental structures of an individual or a group are not too rigid and do not force them overmuch to run away from the real nature of the problem, and above all if that group or individual asks questions, the outcome can be beneficial.

After ten years' research in this field, I am convinced that, however limited the effectiveness of such a process, that is the sole value of what I can offer readers of *Concilium*.

The role of the theologian in this instance is not to supply the answer before the problem is posed. At most the theologian can ask Christians to confirm that there is a problem and that the problem does not necessarily accord with the alleged reasons. Then it is up to the Christians in question to discover the latent content of the problem and to find the solution.

But time is pressing. Not only time but the love of Christ. It would be sad if the men and women of our time passed by Christianity on the assumption that it wasn't even aware of the oddness of its attitude to pleasure. But it would be even more unfortunate if Christians misrepresented the nature of the gospel demands by pretending that the Gospel and only the Gospel explained and justified the Christian attitude to pleasure. Certainly the word of God is uncomfortable and his ways are not our ways. But a symptom is still a symptom, and its oddity is of a different order to the word of God. We now know enough about the Gospel and the symptom not to confuse them.

Translated by V. Green

Notes

1. See on this subject J. E. Kerns, *The Theology of Marriage: The Historical Development of Christian Attitudes Towards Sex and Sanctity in Marriage* (New York, 1964); and J. T. Noonan, *Contraception. A History of its Treatment by the Catholic Theologians and Canonists* (Cambridge, Mass., 1966).

2. That is the process followed by the two abovementioned works.

3. That is what I have done elsewhere. See my *Le Chrétien, le plaisir et la sexualité* (Paris, 1974).

4. *Lumière et Vie* 21 (1974), no. 109: *L'avortement.*

5. There is the idea of sex and pleasure which a Catholic poet like Paul Claudel was able to put forward under the guise of the Gospel in his play *L'Annonce faite à Marie.* I have analyzed it in 'L'Analyse faite a Marie de Paul Claudel', *Etudes freudiennes* (Paris, 1973), nos. 7/8, April, pp. 133-82.

Franz Böckle

The Church and Sexuality

THOSE who have a positive attitude to the Christian faith and the Church will find the articles in this issue quite thought-provoking. All the authors express more or less openly their discontent with the Church's doctrine and teaching on the question of sexuality. The efforts of Vatican II to achieve an integrated view of sexuality has had little effect on the practical aspects of establishing norms of behaviour. The functional purpose of sexuality remains paramount, while the value of sexual desire is acknowledged only grudgingly. This approach relies too heavily on a rigid doctrine, and makes no attempt to come to terms with the incontrovertible evidence of the social sciences.

The articles in this issue contain the warnings of men and women who are experts in their professions as well as being wholehearted members of the Church. Their findings should stimulate us all to think. Nevertheless, a still graver problem is presented by:

I. THE LACK OF CREDIBILITY

There are corresponding indications that the Church's attitude to sexual morality is no longer accepted by a large proportion of its members, especially the younger generation. In short, the Church's doctrine concerning sexuality and marriage is no longer plausible to many of the faithful. The findings of a survey of married couples in Switzerland are further confirmed by surveys conducted in the Federal Republic of Germany. In the 'Survey of all Catholics in preparation for the Joint Synod of all Dioceses in the Federal Republic', 4.5 million of the 21 million questionnaires were returned to the central office (= a return of 25%). A large proportion of the replies came from practising Catholics of whom the majority claimed to have a good to satisfactory relationship with the Church. (55.2% described this relationship as 'good', 30% as 'adequate', and 9.8% as 'disappointing'.) It is extremely interesting to learn what these Catholics expect from their Church in the way of guidance as to how they should model their lives. This must be an approximate indication of the kind and degree of authority which the Church (concretely, the official voice of the Church) still represents for the majority of open-minded Catholics. The answers to the survey show a clear trend. In general terms (question 3: 'What is the purpose of the Church?') altogether two-thirds of the faithful expect some moral guidance ('The Church should further the cause of social justice': 'she should challenge statesmen to peace and justice'). The general assessment of the Church as a moral authority thus appears to be widespread. However, to the more precise question: 'In which areas are the pronouncements of the Church important to you personally?' (question 7), the level of expectancy dropped noticeably. Apparently, the more concrete and personal the sphere in question, the less interest there is in the guiding word of the Church. One third of the faithful still expects meaningful statements from the Church concerning marriage (as an institution) and the bringing up of children. Only 15% of regular church-goers or 10% of a representative cross-section of Catholics still have any such expectations with regard to 'sexual behavior before marriage' or even 'in marriage'. And there was even less desire to be influenced in matters concerning leisure and personal political decisions. A representative survey was carried out to discover more about the background to this general attitude. This revealed a considerable discrepancy between the values held by the faithful and the standpoint adopted by the Church. In order to pick up the finer points of difference the questions were posed in two different forms. In the first instance it was posed objectively, in questionnaire format: 'In which of these areas do you disagree with the standpoint of the Church? Where do you diverge from the teaching of the Church?' The second time a more effective format was chosen: 'In which areas do you encounter problems with the attitude of the Church?' followed by the same list of possibilities. From this it emerged that the strongest feelings of disagreement were definitely experienced in the sphere of sexuality and marriage.

At the top of the list by a considerable margin was the question of birth control (61% disagree, 35% have difficultires). 45% differ on the question of sexuality generally and 39% even on the indissolubility of marriage. A further 22% and 19% respectively encountered "difficulties' on these two points. The fact that these questions should be followed immediately by that concerning the 'authority of the Pope' is in a sense understandable, since papal authority is unfortunately seen by the majority of the faithful solely in the light of the ruling on birth control. A closer examination reveals that the level of disagreement increases with the decline in church attendance. Similarly, it is proportionately higher among the younger generation and the more highly educated.

II. THE CRISIS OF SEXUAL MORALITY

These facts confirm yet again that sexual morality as interpreted by the Church is in a state of crisis. By crisis, of course, I do not mean that valid norms have been transgressed. That has always happened in this sphere as in others. The crisis of morality as interpreted by the Church is due to the widespread and intense criticism currently being levelled at its basic norms. What endangers a moral teaching and its realization is not the fact that its norms should be disregarded so much as that they should be disputed. The nature and cause of this crisis demand careful analysis. A correct diagnosis is vital if moral theology is to succeed in overcoming this crisis in the foreseeable future. The following observations strike me as essential to an understanding of the nature and cause of the crisis:

1) It would seem that what is objected to is not the fundamental value of sexuality and its consequences (i.e. on the behaviour of the individual), but the way in which the specific prohibitions concerning sexuality are justified. The one-sided approach to sexuality is rightly criticised. However, precisely in this respect the teaching of the Church has changed considerably over the past thirty years — as we shall show — though the basic precepts have remained unchanged. The current moral crisis is more a crisis of the authoritative (to a certain extent unfortunately authoritarian) manner in which these precepts are pronounced and justified. This even overshadows the question of their validity. In the Swiss survey mentioned above only about 10% of the married Catholics questioned agreed with the official doctrine that pre-marital sexual relations are 'always sinful'. The percentage of those who considered sex before marriage to be 'right in every case' is also small, whereas by far the largest majority regard this as 'a question for the individual conscience to decide'. As can also be seen from the cross-questions, this does not constitute an outright rejection or denial of the values in question; on the other hand, it does indicate that married Catholics today no longer subscribe to the overall formula 'always sinful' or 'always permissible'. The overwhelming majority of Catholics in the countries where these surveys were conducted are convinced that questions concerning sexual morality should be left to the conscience of the individual. It should be noted that the surveys dealt only with married

Catholics, and these were questioned on their attitude to pre-marital relations. The trend towards responsible decision-making on the part of the individual is now very marked. It is a reaction against any specific form of statutory guidance from outside (the morality of obedience) which for a long time was considered to be symptomatic of the Church's teaching on moral issues. With this kind of morality, the individual is confronted neither by God nor by his fellow-men, but by a system of laws and a corresponding network of sanctions. A moral code of this kind inevitably produces a climate of fear resulting in a wholly negative, defensive battle against any possible loss of social integrity. The growing reluctance to accept the reasons given for such laws and sanctions means that the faithful are beginning more and more to reject this whole method of establishing moral precepts. This is particularly evident in the large percentage of those who disagree with the Church's teaching on birth control. In the case of the younger generation, this rejection is almost universal. There is no longer any sympathy with traditional arguments. On the contrary, there is a widespread demand that such norms be intrinsically plausible, a factor that should be self-evident when moral reason (natural law) is used to justify a prescribed mode of behaviour. In a word, the crisis of morality is not first and foremost a crisis about the values in question, but about the way these values are put across and about the way the norms related to these values are justified.

2) This type of moral crisis clearly has specific social causes. In the first place, the so-called 'open society' with its multiplicity of attitudes. The individual is no longer guided in his behaviour by traditional, entrenched moral values claiming absolute validity, as was the case in the closed 'village community'. In the latter context morality was simply 'what has been passed down over the generations', 'what everyone traditionally' held to be right. Modern man has freed himself from this obligation to tradition. He refuses to toe the line unquestioningly with prescribed modes of behaviour. Instead, he wants to make up his own mind and act according to what he personally feels to be right. This applies in particular — as we shall shortly see — to the most intimate sphere of his existence, his sexuality. Clearly, any personal decision of this kind is influenced by social factors. Instead of being guided by a compulsory code, the individual is now confronted by a wealth of information which gives him the impression that, being well informed, he is able to choose and decide. In reality, it is extremely difficult to evaluate the numerous points of view offered, given the high degree of skilful manipulation of information that operates in the media. What appears to be an autonomous decision is all too often illusory, for we are determined by a whole network of information and motives to a

far greater extent than we imagine. Our moral judgments and decisions are no exception. Hence the crisis of morality also concerns our approach to certain values obscured by social attitudes. This problem obviously cannot be solved merely by insisting on tradition. On the contrary, this would be quite beside the point. The only way of coming to terms with the plurality of diverging opinions is by adopting a constructive but critical approach to the various, often contradictory concepts involved. With regard to sexual norms the situation is further complicated by another factor. In our highly developed industrial society the freedom of the individual is, of necessity, more and more limited by rules, regulations and laws. The *numerus clausus* on university entrants severely restricts the freedom of choice regarding studies and career. The increase in traffic, the threatened shortage of raw materials, the concern with environmental pollution, works councils, and the health service all require progressively stricter organization and control by public and civil institutions. Inevitably, this general restriction of our freedom in society impinges upon the private spheres of marriage, family and sexuality. The widespread need for autonomy in marriage, allowing scope for the individual to shape it according to his wishes, as well as the demand for self-determination of sexual behaviour are to be seen as reactions to the total institutionalization of other aspects of life. What they express is not arbitrariness or immorality but a genuine striving for authenticity. To avoid the danger of total alienation, people are trying to mobilize the dynamic forces of sexuality in a social context. Men and women need each other in order to experience together the discovery of deeper levels of human existence. Clearly, this involves considerable dangers but one should not dismiss the whole development because of the danger of misuse; equally, it would be unjustified to make any generalizations on the basis of isolated cases.

III. PREREQUISITES FOR OVERCOMING THE CRISIS

From this outline of the more important aspects of the crisis in moral teaching it can be seen that the present justification and promulgation of a definite set of basic values is unconvincing. This raises the urgent question as to whether Catholic moral theology is ready and able to overcome this crisis without forfeiting any of its indispensable values, thereby acquiring a new credibility in particular with respect to sexual morality. Some critics are of the opinion that it is already far too late, saying that as far as the younger generation is concerned there is almost no ground left to lose. I disagree! I am convinced that we can still expect a great deal. Indeed, in recent years considerable progress has been made in respect to the problem of norms which could be of real help to us now. In contemporary philosophy the growing insight that many of the seemingly insoluble problems and conflicts of humanity cannot be solved unless there can be some agreement on values has resulted in ethics coming to the forefront of discussion. The first prerequisite is that we know what we want. And if this is not automatically clear, then we have to decide. For this reason intense efforts are being made to overcome the dichotomy between objective knowledge and subjective value judgment, and to create a scientific method for moral arguments. By these means it is hoped to establish to what extent compulsory normative rules can be justified. The moral theologian who follows these endeavours being made by moral philosophy will find them full of stimulating insights forcing him to ever greater precision when justifying moral judgments. In doing so he can refer mainly to his own tradition, as B. Schüller has convincingly proved. But important though it may be to have a formally correct argument to justify a moral judgment, the argument itself must always be based on a solid foundation of reason and conviction. It is essential to make the clear distinction between the origin and development of these insights relating to values and the justification of moral judgments and norms. The two aspects should be neither separated nor fused; they should be viewed singly, and then it should be possible to evaluate to what extent they are interdependent. It is my contention that the current lack of credibility being experienced by the Church is largely due to methodological confusion and incompetence. The Church's pronouncements on sexual morality must be examined along the lines indicated above if moral theology is to regain its power of conviction, indeed if the Church is to regain its credibility.

IV. THE DECISIVE VALUES

In his contribution to this issue, J. Duss-von Werdt points out that sexuality has many different levels of meaning and advocates a 'systematic description of the immense significance of sexuality'. He is critical of the 'one-sided view of sexuality upheld by the official teaching of the Catholic Church with its equation of "sexuality = procreation" (and hence its confinement to the context of marriage)'. He comments that other Council texts adopting a different attitude on this issue have not been taken into consideration. It is essential to establish just what has not been included and why. It seems to me that a number of official post-conciliar documents do in fact manifest a considerable change in their understanding of sexuality. The pastoral letter of the German bishops on 'The Nature and Significance of Sexuality' no longer bears any trace of one-sidedness. Any narrow-minded emphasis on the purely functional aspects of sexuality is dropped completely, and its versatility is explicitly acknowledged. The same applies to the working paper 'Meaning and Structure of Sexuality' prepared by a panel of experts (Committee IV) of the Synod of West German bishops and released for publication by the president of the synod. In this paper it is stated: 'The following factors are significant: (1) Sexuality determines man's whole existence, it forms his maleness or femaleness. (2) Sexuality transmits existential awareness. It offers the individual a means of self-affirmation and of affirmation by his partner. It allocates social roles and furthers the development of the individual. It gives him the experience of sexual desire, of loving his partner, of being accepted by his partner and of expressing this love sexually. It brings him the experience of having and educating children, by whom he is in turn moulded himself. (3) The social significance of human sexuality remains, as always, in the procreation and upbringing of children.' This interpretation of sexuality certainly does not correspond to the general tone of official Church documents. But it is not the only paper of this kind to have appeared since the Council. Its findings reflect the most important discoveries of the social sciences as well as the practical experience of its authors. Its conclusions are by no means novel. For example, the determining factors listed above (the effective and the affective values) are already indicated in writing on marriage prior to the Council. (cf. the article by Pierre de Locht in this issue). The Church's interpretation of sexuality is far more dynamic than is generally supposed. For some time now difficulties have in fact only arisen with respect to the order of precedence of the various values and aims. The Vatican Council deliberately avoided establishing a definite order of preference. The working paper of the German synod referred to above states that sexual behaviour should accommodate the expression and realization of the legitimate interests, wishes and aims of both partners. Allowance should also be made for the social aspects of sexuality. It goes without saying that these factors will not always apply simultaneously. What matters is that love should be 'the unifying and formative principle' determining man's behaviour generally. Again, this sounds convincing, but it is so generalized that the layman might well wonder if anything concrete can be deduced from it, or whether it has any direct bearing on his behaviour. Is the Church prepared to alter its sexual norms as a result of such attitudes as these? It would seem not. As the most recent pronouncements indicate, the Church is determined to persist stubbornly with its traditional norms, according to which sexuality remains bound exclusively within marriage. In other words, sexual intercourse outside or before marriage is still prohibited. Indeed, any attempt to relax the prohibition of contraception was definitively rejected by *Humanae Vitae*. This has caused many of the faithful to part company with us. There is a widespread conviction that the representatives of the Church are prejudiced and unwilling to accept the consequences of these evident changes in moral standards. This has resulted in the atmosphere of conflict outlined above, with many people now living according to their own rules of behaviour.

But is it really inconsequence and perplexity that prevent the Church from adapting its norms? What does this in fact entail? Does it mean that the Church which has always forbidden extra-marital intercourse should now declare that it is permitted? No one would seriously expect that. The working paper prepared by the synod expressly warns against adopting a norm-free moral code. 'The current tendency towards the abolition of existing sexual norms frequently leads to the introduction of new norms. Like the previous set these are based largely on social pressures, even though the symptom is reversed — what was originally forbidden now becomes law.' No responsible decision can be reached without help, and certainly cannot be achieved merely by reducing the existing norms, i.e. by simply shifting the boundaries. 'If the existing standards are no longer convincing, it is often due to the fact that they tend to emphasize one, albeit correct, point of view which they then make into a standard. Morality demands greater flexibility in the decision-making process.' It is hence clear that in view of the many different levels of meaning of sexuality more flexibility in making the necessary decisions is essential, and that help should be given to enable the individual to make these decisions. But it should be stressed that this cannot be achieved either by sweeping away existing norms or by simply shifting the boundaries (i.e. from the marriage ceremony to the promise of marriage). What is needed is clearly not a mere alteration of standards, but an understanding of the nature as well as the obligation of normative declarations *per se*. Furthermore, the origin and justification of moral judgments should be examined. A genuine understanding of the values and aims connected with sexuality does not constitute a moral judgment. What matters in a moral evaluation is solely the free action of the person involved, the act that realizes such values. Until now whenever the decisive values of sexuality were referred to they were depicted as 'pre-moral' values, i.e. as the inherent possibilities of human sexuality. An understanding of such values is doubtless of fundamental importance for the moral estimation of actions. But since we are dealing exclusively with contingent values, the moral estimation of an action can only be evaluated by taking account of the relative conditions of the value, and by comparing it with any other possible values. Although the absolute value of morals makes unconditional demands of man, as a contingent being in a contingent world he can never fully realize the one *bonum* or good demanded of him; instead, he is limited to contingent or 'relative' values or *bona*, the highest value being by definition unattainable. Hence all that remains is to establish which is the most worthy of these values, and this means that every concrete categorical decision *must* —to avoid making an absolute of the wrong chance connection — in the final analysis be based on a choice of merit in which the highest value is binding. In this way the moral relevance of contingent values is *not* contested, but merely prevented from being falsely raised to the status of an absolute. For only the *bonum*, i.e. God himself, can make absolute demands.

From this we can see what it means when a categoric moral act is judged as such (*in se, intrinsece*) to be good or bad. That is to say, that this act is determined by an objective value content. But since every value created is conditional, likewise a moral judgment is only valid if the conditions of the relevant value are fulfilled. This sounds commonplace, and indeed a reading of Suarez's *De Legibus* demonstrates that none of this is new to moral theology. But if we then open *Humanae Vitae*, no. 14, we read that sexual intercourse rendered deliberately infertile is an intrinsically immoral act (*intrinsece inhonestum*), and that it is 'never permitted — no matter how grave the reasons — to do wrong for a good purpose, i.e. to want something that inherently offends the moral code'. This latter point is right in the sense that no intention, no matter how good, can ever justify a morally bad action. *The question is whether the intentionally infertile sexual act is unconditionally wrong in moral terms.* This is not explicitly stated in the text, but it is insinuated that the concept *intrinsece inhonestum* is to be understood to mean 'unconditional — absolutely contrary to morality', because the ultimate point of the argument is to forbid artificial contraception in any circumstances, with no regard whatever for any possible consequences. This constitutes what is referred to in contemporary moral theology as de-ontological establishing of norms, a term corresponding to the *moralitas absoluta* in handbooks. It is generally agreed among moral theologians that this method of establishing norms represents a rare exception in the otherwise almost consistently teleological (i.e. taking into account the consequences of an action) arguments employed in the Catholic tradition. Recent enquiries rightly dispute the de-ontological justification of moral judgments concerning categoric acts. Only analytical judgments can claim deontological validity (to murder, i.e. to kill unjustly, is unjust!). Whoever recognizes the contingency of the values determining our human actions must be in favour of considering that prerequisites for an evaluation of good. This applies to all contingent 'goods', including the good of procreation. But even here we cannot say that there could never be a greater good and that it is therefore absolutely binding — as is implied in the norms applied in the case of birth control. In permitting the regulation of fertility by the choice of time, the relative value of procreation has already been indirectly admitted. But in order to maintain the immorality of using contraceptives *Humanae Vitae* resorts to the concept of God's will as manifested in the natural law ('Deus . . . naturales leges ac tempora fecunditatis . . . disposuit'). Moral judgments are no longer based solely on value judgments; rather, responsible human action is bound to the maintenance of biological laws. This was subject to hefty criticism from many sides after *Humanae Vitae*, but we do not want to repeat what has already been said many times before. However, it should be emphasized that this criticism constitutes a questioning of values unprecedented in Catholic tradition. Tradition rightly judges human actions according to objective value judgments, but in this instance the determining factor is not a value judgment but the difference between a natural and an artificial cause. A biological fact is declared to be the norm, surely a strange way of saving a de-ontological argument that cannot be upheld on the basis of the value of procreation itself.

What follows from these considerations? That all moral judgments of sexual behavior are teleologically founded, i.e. that they are based on the evaluation of the various relevant values. Norms, concrete laws or bans are the generalized expression of such judgments. This does not make them any less binding, but their validity depends on the correctness of the underlying moral evaluation which must be continually reviewed. If this is assessed correctly, we can say that the dynamism of sexual morality is acknowledged. This does not mean that we advocate giving up norms, or disregarding obligation in a purely subjective manner. But we do demand that value judgments that were once possibly well-founded should be re-examined. A couple of examples should make this clear. A teleological justification of the moral judgment underlying the traditional ban on contraception would have to be on the following lines: 'It is immoral to actively exclude procreation from the sexual act unless there are important reasons for avoiding a pregnancy and abstinence is detrimental to the well-being of the couple.' Conditions have changed so much today that morally justifiable contraception proves the rule rather than the exception. But this does not mean that the moral judgment should be altered, although the change in practice should also be reflected in formative terms. This could be achieved by declaring that contraception should be justified in each individual case, and that the particular method employed should take full consideration of the health and personal dignity of the partners. The statements issued by a number of recent synods all point in this direction. The situation as far as the prohibition of extra-marital and pre-marital sexual intercourse is concerned is in some respects easier and in other respects more difficult to assess. From the moral theologian's point of view the problem is simpler, because the condemnation of *fornicatio simplex* (extra-marital intercourse) has always been teleologically substantiated. According to Liguori it is based on the supposition that it represented a general danger. Subsequently, this argument gave rise to continued discussion about the possibility of justified exceptions, for the argument *ex periculo communi* is hardly suited to exclude every exception as morally tenable. Vermeersch recognized this danger, among others, as did Tamburini and Bellerini before him. He thus attempted to justify the ban according to the basic order of things. This basic order of things, which must be acknowledged as God's order, can be deduced by generalizing and abstracting experience. It is not necessary to take this discussion any further. It cannot be disputed that theological arguments have traditionally been applied in this connection and that any possible exceptions have been discussed on the basis of an evaluation of their respective merit. But it is far more difficult to decide whether the conditions originally thought to engender this general danger have now changed so radically that every exception imaginable is automatically to be regarded as normal. Many people are of the opinion that a genuine understanding of the values associated with human sexuality would demand that greater emphasis be laid on the actual experience of love between partners, and that this would inevitably entail a reduction of emphasis on the institutional aspect. On the other hand, it should be made clear that the best chance of achieving a mutual love relationship based on a fulfilled sexual relationship is in marriage itself. The institutional element is by no means insignificant. In addition, the question of pre- or extra-marital relations among Christians can only be examined and assessed in the context of the indissoluble obligation of faithfulness in marriage. Any assessment of the potential human value of sexuality necessarily entails a totally different appreciation of pre- and extra-marital sexuality. But if this evaluation means drawing in the dignity and indissolubility of sacramental marriage, and permanent sexual happiness within marriage, then clearly freedom in the pre- or extra-marital sphere is strictly limited.

These few remarks on practical questions are in no way intended to be understood as the moral assessment of the problems themselves. For that it would be necessary to examine in detail the debatable value of each individual question. In addition, social and historico-cultural factors would have to be taken into consideration. It is the aim of this article to investigate the fundamental basis and method for judging sexual behaviour according to the criteria of moral theology. These basic reflections can be summarized as follows:

1) The moral judgment of sexual behaviour is connected with value judgments. Since these values are contingent, no single value can unconditionally determine our actions. Hence, in the final analysis, the judgment is based on a relative evaluation of the values in question.

2) Teleologically justified norms are by no means subjectively adaptable. On the contrary, they are universally binding. However, 'universality' signifies 'generally valid', i.e. the norms are valid so long as they express the general will and so far as they encompass and give adequate consideration to the revelant conditions.

3) The official teaching of such norms does not remove their hypothetical character. For this to happen, the Church would have to declare some contingent value to be absolute. The stated priority of one specific value over others (*finis primarius*!) does not alter the fact that it is inherently contingent provided, that is, that even a possible revelation would not alter the logical structure of the moral norms.

4) This does not exclude the fact that certain categorical values are particularly moulded by the Christian approach to faith. Hence we cannot let things rest with a mere negative statement (the non-changeability of the categoric structure of morality), since precisely this overlooks the intrinsic possibilities of ecclesiastical pronouncement on the subject. In view of the expectations directed towards the encyclical *Humanae Vitae*, it is hardly surprising that the papal statement was interpreted as adopting a definite normative attitude, thereby provoking a negative or, worse still, an indifferent reaction. The rejection of the Pope's inconsistent attempt to justify his position in this matter inevitably entails a regrettable degree of indifference towards his other noteworthy statements on the overall meaning of human sexuality. Precisely here, in the process of creating and strengthening moral judgments that precede all questions of ethical justification, would be the place for an independent contribution to the spreading of the faith. Our concern here is to implant ethical value judgments in the fundamental view of world and man, in the previously assumed system of values which is itself transmitted by various processes. This is where the Church's main opportunity lies to make a specific contribution. For, on the basis of its faith, the Church can contribute decisively to the true picture of man, and hence to an appropriate way for man to achieve self-realization. If this teaching is not prematurely combined with an inappropriate model norm, the Church will have a far greater chance of having its moral teaching heard and accepted, and so bring the values it regards as essential into the process of establishing relative values. In this way Catholic sexual morality could be far more

dynamic.

Translated by Sarah Twohig

Contributors

FRANZ BÖCKLE is professor of moral theology at Bonn University. Among his publications are *Gesetz und Gewissen* (1965) and other works on natural law, fundamental moral theology, and conscience.

JACQUES-MARIE POHIER, O.P., is vice-rector of the Saulchoir Faculties and professor there. He has published several books and articles on psychology and theology, including *Psychologie et Théologie* (1967) and *Au nom du Père: Recherches théologiques et psychoanalytiques* (1972).

PETER GO is a Carmelite, born in Surabaya (Indonesia) in 1937. He pursued his studies at the Batu-Malang College of Philosophy and Theology and at the University of Mainz. Since then he has undertaken further study at the University of Bonn and has been active in pastoral work among students and parishioners.

PIERRE DE LOCHT is a lecturer at the University of Louvain and is a member of the national board of the Centre d'Education à la Famille et à l'Amour. Since 1946 he has been actively involved in the family apostolate and has written many articles devoted to the twin issues of moral theology and family life.

KAJETAN KRIECH is a Capuchin, ordained in 1955. Since 1964 he has been an instructor in moral theology at the Capuchin house for theological study in Solothurn (Switzerland). He has published articles on moral theology in various journals.

MARGARETA ERBER is ordinary professor of biology at Paderborn Central College. She received a doctorate in the natural sciences with a thesis on the biological concept of potency (Trier, 1971). More recently she has been interested in comparing data and findings of the various biological disciplines, particularly insofar as they have implications for anthropology.

MARIE AUGUSTA NEAL has taught sociology at the University of California at Berkeley and at Harvard University. She is a past president of the Association for Sociology of Religion and has been a member of the Advisory Board of the USCC. She is the author of *Values and Interests in Social Change* (1965) and of numerous articles.

JEAN LEMAIRE is a psychiatrist and a psychoanalyst. He is assistant director of the University of Paris V and the founder and former president of the Association Française des Centres de Consultation Conjugale. He is also the editorial director of the periodical *Dialogue: Etudes et recherches sur les problèmes du couple.* He is the author of *Les Thérapies du Couple* (1971) and has collaborated on an anthology which is soon to be published, *De la thérapie du couple à la thérapie par le couple.*

EVELYNE LEMAIRE-ARNAULD, a psychoanalyst, is a therapist at the Centre Hospitalier de Versailles. She is in charge of supervised projects at the University of Paris V and is also an executive on the research commission of the Association Française des Centres de Consultation Conjugale. In collaboration with Jean Lemaire she wrote *Les Conflits Conjugaux* (1966).

KLAUS BREUNING, ordained in 1953, is a teacher of religion on the high school level. He is also the director of studies and professional seminars in the Osnabrück (West Germany) public school system. His publications include *Die Vision des Reiches: Deutscher Katholizismus zwischen Demokratie und Diktatur* (1969) and *Worte zum Alltag* (1973). He has also contributed many articles dealing with religious education and sex education.